CONTENTS

INTRODUCTION

CHRISTMAS IS A CRAZY TIME OF YEAR, WHEN REINDEER FLY THROUGH THE SKY. NO ONE EVER STOPS TO WONDER WHAT HAPPENS WHEN DANCER OR PRANCER WANT A POOP.

YOU DON'T WANT TO BE STANDING UNDERNEATH WHEN THEY DO A DOO-DOO, DO YOU? MAYBE THE BEST CHRISTMAS PRESENT WOULD BE UMBRELLAS FOR EVERYONE?

Or what if a present fell off Father Christmas's sleigh? You're hurrying home, tired after a Christmas carol service and a bike lands on your head. You'd be tyred all right.

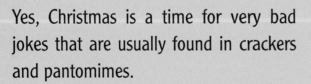

REINDEER DROPPINGS MAYBE, BUT AT LEAST THERE'S NO CHANCE OF BEING HIT BY A BICYCLE DROPPING FROM THE SKY

CLANG!

SPOKE TOO SOON ... SPOKE... GET IT?

Yes, Christmas is a time for very bad jokes that are usually found in crackers and pantomimes.

But Christmas has always been a dangerous time. History is full of horrible things that have happened in the season of peace and goodwill. This is a **BIG FAT BOOK** full of fat, foul facts about the terrors of the Christmas period.

Christmas and curses

Of course Christmas isn't just one disastrous day, it's a season. There are, as I'm sure you've heard in the carol, **twelve days of Christmas**.

And even if you survive twelve days you aren't safe. You have to take down your Christmas decorations on the twelfth day of Christmas, the night of 5 January, or you bring disaster on your house.

'WHY DO YOU HAVE TO TAKE DOWN CHRISTMAS DECORATIONS', YOU CRY? I'M GLAD YOU ASKED.

- Long ago, people believed that tree spirits lived in the holly and the ivy that was used to decorate houses at Christmas.

- Kind people took the tree spirits into the house to stop them freezing in the winter weather.

- But those tree spirits are needed outside to make sure things grow in the spring. They can't do that if they are trapped in your house, can they?

7

- No springtime means no crops, so everyone starves. All because YOU left up your Christmas decorations.

- And if those spirits are stuck in your bedroom (under that pile of smelly socks in the corner) they will start to make mischief. They'll probably play tricks on you.

WHAT SORT OF TRICKS, YOU ASK? OH, I DON'T KNOW...

IF YOU TRAPPED ME IN YOUR BEDROOM (UNDER THE SMELLY SOCKS) I WOULD HIDE YOUR HOMEWORK SO YOU WOULD GET INTO TROUBLE WHEN YOU GO BACK TO SCHOOL. TEACHER WOULD GIVE YOU DETENTION FOR THE REST OF YOUR LIFE AND THAT WOULD SERVE YOU RIGHT FOR TRAPPING ME.

You see what I mean? Christmas is a dangerous time and always has been. You need a book that tells you of all the dangers of Christmas time. All about the horrible things that have happened in history. That way you can save yourself from the worst disasters.

YOU LUCKY, LUCKY PERSON. YOU HAVE THAT BOOK IN YOUR HANDS RIGHT NOW. READ ON.

25
DECEMBER

ON THE FIRST DAY OF CHRISTMAS,
THE RATTUS SENT TO ME . . .
A HORR-I-BLE HIS-TOR-EE

MAGIC AND MISSIONARIES

HORRIBLE HISTORIES
MESSAGE:

This is a
'HORRIBLE HISTORIES'
SPECIAL book.

'WHAT'S SO SPECIAL ABOUT IT?' YOU ASK. YOU'RE AN IMPATIENT ONE, AREN'T YOU? TURN THE PAGE AND I'LL TELL YOU...

11

This book is special because it's written by a Rattus — one of the creatures that has been around in history as long as humans can remember.

Just look at him — as handsome a chap as you'd ever wish to meet in a churchyard at midnight.

WE RATS MAKE IT OUR BUSINESS TO BE THERE AT ALL THE HORRIBLE EVENTS IN HISTORY, AND AS A CHRISTMAS RATTUS I'M THE BEST PERSON TO SHARE ALL THE FASCINATING FACTS ABOUT THE FESTIVE TIME OF THE YEAR. YOU WOULD NOT BE-*LIEVE* THE THINGS I'VE SEEN.

LET'S START AT THE VERY BEGINNING OF HISTORY WHEN I WAS A YOUNG RAT-LET AND YOU HUMANS WERE NOT MUCH MORE THAN MONKEYS.

CHRISTMAS CELEBRATES THE BIRTHDAY OF JESUS OF COURSE, BUT PEOPLE WERE HAVING WINTER PARTIES LONG BEFORE JESUS WAS BORN TWO THOUSAND YEARS AGO. THOSE PARTY DAYS MUST HAVE STARTED IN THE STONE AGE ...

Stone-age strife

As winter comes, the days get shorter. The stone-agers must have huddled around their fires in their cold caves and worried.

And that's what they did. They lit big fat fires. They thought the magic would work. And if they lit the fire on 21 December – the shortest day of the year – it always did. From then on the days get longer.

1. You can read more about the cave people in *Horrible Histories Savage Stone Age*.

Then, around 2,000 years ago, the Christians went around preaching about Jesus. They told the story of His birth in a stable, and the shepherds and wise men bringing gifts.

The Christian missionaries met people who believed in other gods – people like:

• **the Celts who had gods who lived in rivers and trees**

• **the Greeks who had gods that lived on a mountain**

• **the Romans who had gods that lived everywhere from door hinges to fireplaces, and from cupboards to mouldy weeds. (Honest.)**

How did the Christians get these people to give up their old gods?

Of course the 25 December is four days after the shortest day but it's near enough.

People started to like Christmas so they made their parties last for 12 days – the 12 days of Christmas.

NOW LISTEN UP, THIS IS HARD TO GET YOUR BRAIN CELL AROUND. THE FIRST 'DAY' OF CHRISTMAS IS 26 DECEMBER. BUT ... THE 'DAY' IN ANCIENT TIMES STARTED AT SUNSET THE EVENING BEFORE. SO THE 'FIRST DAY OF CHRISTMAS' STARTS AT SUNSET ON 25 DECEMBER OR 26 DECEMBER OR BOTH. GOT THAT? I HOPE YOU UNDERSTAND IT BECAUSE I DO ... MAYBE.

The Twelve Days of Christmas and their customs

THROUGHOUT HISTORY THERE HAVE BEEN LOTS OF CURIOUS CHRISTMAS CUSTOMS. THE ONE YOU LIKE BEST IS THE CUSTOM OF GIVING PRESENTS TO CHILDREN ON CHRISTMAS DAY ...
    BUT DID YOU KNOW THAT CHILDREN IN OTHER PLACES AND OTHER TIMES SOMETIMES GOT PRESENTS ON A DIFFERENT DAY? THERE ARE OTHER QUAINT CUSTOMS ON THE TWELVE DAYS TOO ...

16

• In Spain, and Spanish South America, 28 December is a day for tricks ... rather like April Fool's Day in other countries. The Bible says that when Jesus was born, King Herod ordered the killing of all the innocent children around Bethlehem, so 28 December is known as 'Massacre of the Innocents Day'. The people who suffer the tricks played on this day are called 'innocents'.

YOUR TRICK VICTIMS ... OR TRICKTIMS ... ARE NOT ALLOWED TO GET ANNOYED WITH YOU, BUT I'D BE FURIOUS IF YOUR TRICK WAS TO DROP A BRICK ON MY HEAD.

• In the Middle Ages you would see what day 28 December falls on. If it's (say) a Tuesday then you have a day off EVERY Tuesday for the year until next Innocents' Day. King Louis XI of France followed that custom. He had a day off every week and his ministers were scared to speak to him on that day if some urgent problem came along.

• On New Year's Eve in Scotland, there is an old custom called 'first-footing'. New Year strikes. The first person to enter your house after that is important. They should carry a lump of coal – that means you will never be cold all year. They should carry a small cake – that means you'll never go hungry (unless a rat gets the cake first). And they'll carry a coin so you'll never be poor ... unless you drop it down the back of the settee.

knocked down your door that meant bad luck – no food, no fuel, no money for you because the vicious Vikings would nick it all. If your first-footer is dark-haired with a coal-covered cake and a crumb-covered coin then welcome them in. If they step inside, pull out a sword and chop you, then they are probably a Viking in a dark wig.

The odd thing is that this visitor has to be dark haired. Why? Some clever people say it all goes back to the days when fair-haired Vikings raided Scotland. If they

25 DECEMBER
On this horrible day in history ...

1066

William the Conqueror, the Norman Duke, has smashed the Saxons at the Battle of Hastings on 14 October. He heads for London to be crowned but halfway there, at Canterbury, William and his soldiers fall sick from the disease of dysentery. They have a fever, diarrhoea with blood, and vomiting. Some will die. William lives. Welcome to England, William.

After a l-o-n-g and s-l-o-w march he reaches London to be crowned.

For the coronation, on Christmas Day, William invites French-speaking Normans and English-speaking Saxons.

The crown is put on his head and the guests in Westminster Abbey shout and cheer – a babble of voices in both languages.

The Norman soldiers, who are on guard outside, think the noise inside is the Saxons

trying to murder William. The soldiers begin setting fire to the houses around the Abbey. (No, I agree, that doesn't make a lot of sense – they think their king is being killed in the Abbey so they run off and set fire to houses? Weird, but it's what the history books say.)

The fire spreads from house to house. Smoke fills the church, the guests flee and riots break out in the streets of London. Back inside the Abbey, William and the priests finish the service, in spite of all the chaos. But a bishop writes,

'William trembled from head to foot.'

No more Mr Tough-Guy, eh? Happy Christmas, wobbling William.[2]

2. Read more about William and the Normans in *Horrible Histories Stormin' Normans*.

26
DECEMBER

On the second day of Christmas,
the Rattus sent to me ...
two bombs a-dropped,
and a horr-i-ble his-tor-ee.

DEADLY DRAMA

CHRISTMAS IS THE TIME OF YEAR WHEN THERE IS A SPECIAL TYPE OF PLAY AT THE THEATRE. A PANTOMIME – FULL OF COLOUR AND NOISE, SILLY SONGS AND VERY BAD JOKES. THERE ARE WICKED VILLAINS, (OH YES THERE ARE) AND HANDSOME HEROES IN DREADFUL DANGER ... HE'S BEHIND YOU!

23

There are comical women (played by men) and handsome men (played by women). It's a world turned upside down and you'd usually only see it at Christmas.

In the Second World War (1939 to 1945) a lot of fun had disappeared. Guy Fawkes bonfires were banned because of the 'Blackout' ... and the German bombers dropped much nastier fireworks anyway. Summer holidays for workers in the factories were short because they were needed to make the bullets and bombs. Chocolate was hard to get so Easter eggs vanished. But Christmas fun was still around.

In 1940, bombing stopped from Christmas Eve till 27 December and pantomimes continued to raise people's spirits.

Here is a play for you to perform with your friends – the sort you may have seen when the British were being bombed in the Blitz. The war was no joke ... but the pantomime probably had enough bad jokes in it to cheer you up...

BLITZED BRIT PANTO

SCENE 1:
A cottage in the woods

Narrator: In a crumbling cottage on the edge of Forest Gloom lived the poor but lovely Gretel. (*Enter GRETEL RRH.*) Gretel was young but she was brave, and she joined the Red Cross to nurse our wounded troops. Her uniform was a red cloak. From that day she was known as Gretel Red Riding Hood. She lived in the cottage with her poor but dishonest mother, Mother Hubbard. (*Enter MOTHER HUBBARD with washing basket. GRETEL skips while Mother Hubbard pegs large £5 notes to the washing line to dry.*)

Gretel RRH: Old Mother Hubbard, went to her cupboard,
To get her poor doggy a plum.
When she got there, the cupboard was bare,
So the dog took a bite of her bum!

Mother H: I'll give you plums, my girl! My cupboard's so bare even

25

the mice have moved out! It's because all our food is rationed. All we have is whale meat. **(1)**

Gretel RRH: Not again!

Mother H: Yes ... (*sings to the tune of 'We'll Meet Again'*) Whale meat again, don't know where, don't know when! **(2)**

Mother H & Gretel RRH: (*together*) But there'll be real meat again, some sunny day.

Gretel RRH: Never mind, Mum, this war can't go on forever. Something will turn up, it always does. That reminds me, I used my last sweetie coupon to buy Granny a bar of chocolate. I thought I'd take it to her. She hasn't been well.

Mother H: You're a good girl. You

run off to Granny's ... but watch out for wicked men in the woods!

Gretel RRH: Wicked men! What wicked men?

Mother H: They reckon that Mr Hitler is dropping men from the sky with parachutes. That's why I joined the Local Defence Volunteers (*bravely*) ... we old may be too old to fight, but we can all do our bit by joining the LDV to watch for enemy invaders! Join your local LDV ... now! **(3)**

Gretel RRH: LDV! The girls at school say it stands for 'Look ... duck ... and vanish'! They call them Dad's Army!

Mother H: Less of your cheek girl! Away with you ... and give Granny my love!

(Exit)

SCENE 2:
Deep in the woods

Gretel RRH: (*Terribly upbeat*) I'm sure there are none of Mr Hitler's nasty men in the woods!

Rudolf: (*Steps out of shadows. He is dressed as a nun*). I wonder if you could help me. I am looking for the local tank factory. (*Aside*) I plan to blow it up. **(4)**

Gretel RRH: My Granny is the factory caretaker! Take the next left fork and you're there!

Rudolf: That's all I wanted to know! So, if I get rid of your Granny and take her place I can get in and destroy it! (*Grabs her and begins to tie her to a tree.*)

Gretel RRH: Oh, my, Mr Spy! What a big nose you have!

Rudolf: All the better to see you with!

Gretel RRH: Oh, no! What have I done? The posters all tell us ... careless talk costs lives! Miss Leaky Mouth should have kept her leaky mouth shut! **(5)** Help! Oh, help!

(*Hansel enters, in uniform. He is limping heavily, but bravely. Rudolf hides behind the tree.*)

Hansel: That's the lovely young woman who nursed me in the hospital last week! The moment I saw her I fell in love with her! (*To Gretel RRH.*) Young lady! Why are you so upset?

Gretel RRH: That's the handsome young soldier I nursed in the hospital last week! The moment I saw him I fell in love with him. (*To Hansel*) My hero! Set me free, catch the enemy spy and stop his evil game! (*Hansel sees Rudolf. They fight a comic fight. Rudolf ends up tied to the tree and Gretel RRH is free*)

Gretel RRH: I'm free. But I am still so very poor! Father died a war hero and we have no one to earn us any money.

Hansel: But I am rich. Darling! Marry me! I could sing with happiness! (*Enter Mother H looking sickened by this display of love*)

Mother H: You both make me want to throw up! Now get away to Granny's cottage Red Riding Hood. (*To Hansel*) And you, young man, can share a cup of acorn coffee with me while we talk about your wedding plans. I've got an old parachute that'll make a lovely dress ... (*leads Hansel off*)

Narrator: So Hansel and Gretel Red Riding Hood married and lived happily ever after.

Rudolf: What about me?

Narrator: Rudolf the Spy? He was shot for spying **(6)**.

Rudolf: What?

Narrator: No ... shot. The end.

Rudolf: It certainly is.

APPLAUSE

Panto foul facts

(1) You could only buy food if you had a Ration Book with cut-out coupons. You had to hand over the coupons, with your money, to get food … but you didn't get a lot of food each week. And sometimes it was hard to get good food. People in the Second World War really DID eat whale meat and blubber … well, you'd blubber too if you had to eat whale meat.

(2) Soldiers went off to war and left their families behind. Soppy songs were very popular and the top pop song started like this: 'We'll meet again, don't know where, don't know when, but I know we'll meet again some sunny day…' The lucky ones DID get to meet again, but not all of them.

(3) British people were sure Hitler's armies would attack Britain. The first attacks would come from soldiers dropped on parachutes, so they thought. They also believed the enemy soldiers would disguise themselves as nuns, though they never did. The LDV changed its name to 'The Home Guard' but everyone called them 'Dad's Army'. Their main job was to look out for the enemies on parachutes. A lot of Dad's Army died or were badly hurt in the war through accidents. The clumsy riflemen sometimes shot their friends or themselves by mistake.

WHEN ON GUARD DUTY IT PAYS TO REMEMBER TO WEAR YOUR GLASSES

(4) The Germans DID send spies to Britain but they were all caught and never did any damage.

(5) The British put up posters warning people not to talk to strangers because they could be spies. A poster saying 'Careless talk costs lives' was everywhere. And a woman who DID talk was called 'Miss Leaky Mouth'.

(6) Some Germans were caught spying in Britain. They were executed by hanging or, sometimes, shooting.[3]

You never know who's listening!

CARELESS TALK COSTS LIVES

3. Read more about the war in *Horrible Histories Woeful Second World War*.

Lion around

Queen Victoria (born 1819 – died 1901) was not a great fan of pantomimes. 'It was noisy and nonsensical as usual,' she whinged one year.

But she did like the lion tamer's act. The tamer was called Van Amburgh, a cross-eyed man from America. Victoria wrote in her diary …

> He takes them by their paws, throws them down, makes them roar and lies upon them. It is quite beautiful to see and makes me wish I could do the same.

The queen was such a fan that she watched the act six times in six weeks. One part of the act saw a lamb placed in the cage with the lions. Van Amburgh would tell them not to eat it. On one night the lions behaved and didn't touch the lamb … but a leopard was less polite. That leopard must have been the black sheep of the wild cats. Van Amburgh had to rescue the lamb from the leopard's jaws.

It excited the queen who said it was 'beautiful and wonderful' to watch the rescue. Not if you were a suffering sheep, Vic. Baa.

WE WERE QUITE AMUSED

26 DECEMBER
On this horrible day in history ...

1846

81 Americans have been trying to cross the country to start a new life in the West. They are called The Donner Party. Some have already died of disease during the long journey. They were meant to have reached the awesome Sierra Nevada Mountains by September but the trail has been tough. There are no roads. They often have to clear a path as they trudge along. They have been arguing among themselves and one man has murdered another in a fight. An old

man is told to walk because the horses are too weak to carry him. A couple of days later the old man's feet split open – he is never seen again.

By November they have this last range of mountains to cross – the pioneers have almost made it in their

wagons when they reach the Sierra Nevadas. One last barrier but a tough one. And because it has taken them so long they have eaten the cattle and corn they brought with them. Native Americans have stolen a lot of horses and cattle too. And, of course, the winter is closing in around them.

It snows … and snows … and snows a lot more. Snowdrifts are three metres high. The pioneers are trapped in the snow with no food. On the 26 December, 17 men, women and children set out on snow shoes to get to the warmer coast on the far side of the mountains. In that group eight die in that cruel Christmas. The other

nine eat them. Well, it makes a change from cold turkey on Boxing Day doesn't it? Two helpful members of the Miwok tribe come to guide them to safety – the pioneers shoot them and munch on Miwok muscles.

36 of the pioneers who stayed behind will die. The survivors will finally be led to safety in February 1847.[4]

4. Read more about the troubles of the American settlers in *Horrible Histories USA*.

27
DECEMBER

ON THE THIRD DAY OF CHRISTMAS,
THE RATTUS SENT TO ME...
THREE ROASTED DORMICE,
TWO BOMBS A-DROPPED,
AND A HORR-I-BLE HIS-TOR-EE.

FOUL FOOD

I LOVE FOOD, ME. I LIKE FAST FOOD ... I GRAB IT FROM YOUR DUSTBIN AND I EAT IT FAST BEFORE NEXT-DOOR'S CAT GETS IT. OR BEFORE NEXT-DOOR'S CAT GETS ME FOR CHRISTMAS DINNER.

A Christmas feast

King Charles II was given a Christmas dinner to remember in 1660. The menu contained more than forty dishes, including …

A COLLAR OF BRAWN (meat from a pig's head that's sometimes known as 'head cheese')

A SWAN ROAST

A YOUNG KID

A BOILED PARTRIDGE

SIX EELS

A DISH OF LARKS

POWDERED GEESE JELLIES

You will be sorry to know the partridge was not in a pear tree.

I'M NOT SORRY, WHO WANTS THEIR BRANCHES SAT ON BY A SOGGY PARTRIDGE?

A YOUNG KID? DON'T WORRY, THAT'S A BABY GOAT … NOT ONE OF YOU LOT

Rowdy Romans

THE ROMANS PROBABLY STARTED THE WINTER-FEAST IDEA OF HAVING HOLLY IN THE HOUSE TO KEEP OUT 'THE EVIL EYE'

Holly was supposed to guard the house against:

poison 💀
storms ☁️
fire

In December, the Romans gathered holly in the temples of Saturn – one of their gods. They honoured Saturn with raucous parties and a lot of food!

DID YOU KNOW?

• Roman masters would hold a feast for Saturn called Saturnalia and they would serve food to the slaves. How kind. But the slaves still had to cook it. And THEN the slaves had to serve the master's dinner, as usual. Not much of a treat.

• There were gifts during Saturnalia too. Romans burned sacrifices in the temple and had parties, two hundred years before the first Christmas. In Roman Britain the Saturnalia feast day was held on 25 December. The Christians just changed the Saturnalia feast to Christmas – and their flaming sacrifice was a Christmas Pudding.

• During the Saturnalia celebrations, people ate the most putrid party food. See if you fancy any of these delightful Roman delicacies for your Christmas dinner: ostrich brains. No? How about snails fattened in milk and blood? Or maybe some tasty little dormice, stuffed and roasted with honey? Mmmm, yum! The slaves got bread and cheese as usual.

• While the poor people were having their parties the posh were plotting. In 63 BC the Romans had no emperors. A group of men called senators ran the country. One of them, the crafty Catiline, planned to murder all the other senators and make himself the top man. His gang of plotters would set fire to Rome during Saturnalia while the Romans were too stuffed to stop them. But a girlfriend of one of the gang betrayed them and Catiline had to run from Rome. His army was defeated by the Roman army and Catiline died fighting. The other plotters were executed.

• Saturn was the Roman name for a god the Greeks called Cronus. The legends say Cronus ate his children to stop them from taking his throne. (Don't tell your Dad or it may give him ideas about how to save on your pocket money.)[5]

• Saturn gave his name to Saturday ... a day you always have off school. You really should make a sacrifice to Saturn to say 'Thank you.' Perhaps you could burn your teacher's smelly socks.

5. Read more about the Romans in *Horrible Histories Rotten Romans*.

Awful Arthur

King Arthur and the Knights of the Round Table have had many stories told about them. One legend says Arthur spent Christmas in York in 521. He and his family and friends had so much to eat and drink the monks said that they forgot the true meaning of Christmas and went back to the Roman ways.

The writer said:

'They spent the end of December in laughter, fun, and drunkenness. The pagan winter feasts to Saturn were remembered, but there were twice as many in Arthur's day. Among the rich people there were three times as many.'

Rich people enjoying laughter, fun, and drunkenness while the poor shiver in their huts. Not much changes in 1,500 years, does it?

Boar draw

In the Middle Ages the big Christmas treat was a roasted boar's head. As the old joke says …

Yes, you would sit at the table and see a pig's head staring back at you. Why? Boars were vicious creatures – they were a sign of war and some lords painted a boar on their shields to show how tough they were.

To kill a boar was seen as a great and brave thing to do, so a boar was a fitting sacrifice to make at ancient winter feasts… until guns were invented. (Pig versus gun is not a fair fight.)

In the Middle Ages, a decorated boar's head would carried into the dining-room of a lord with a great show.

The taste for serving a boar's head on Christmas Day went on until the Puritans took power in the 1640s and they banned not just the boar's head custom, but Christmas itself!

We still remember the old beheaded boar custom today when we buy a ham at Christmas.

Gruesome game

Old customs like boar-hunting were taken around the world when the British Empire began to spread. Boar-hunting in India was known by brutal Brits as 'pig sticking'.

GREAT FUN ... UNLESS YOU HAPPEN TO BE A PIG. IF YOU ARE THEN LOOK AWAY NOW.

The 'pigs' were wild boars, and they were hunted by wildly boar-ing men like Robert Baden-Powell. This great chap is remembered today because he founded the Boy Scouts. Lord pig-sticking Powell wrote a book about his gory boar games ...

Pig-Sticking

THE BOAR

The boar is brave and tough, as fast as a horse, and can jump where a horse cannot. He stands as high as a table, is long in the leg, and very muscular. He doesn't hesitate to swim a river, even when it is inhabited by crocodiles.

Well, that is the fellow we hunt in India on horseback with spears, and there is no sport can touch hog-hunting for excitement or valuable training.

THE HUNT

Three or four riders form a 'party.' Beaters drive the pig out of his lair in the jungle, and the party then race after him, but for the first three-quarters of a mile he can generally outrun them.

The honours then go to the man who can first catch and spear him. But as soon as the boar finds himself in danger of being overtaken he either 'jinks,' that is, darts off sideways, or else turns round and charges his pursuer.

A spear-thrust, unless delivered in a vital spot, has little effect beyond making him more angry, and then follows a good deal of charging on both sides, and it is not always the boar that comes off second best.

He has a wonderful power of quick and effective use of his tusks and many a good horse has been fatally gashed by the animal he was hunting.

Noel nosh

• After years of posh people hunting them down there weren't a lot of wild boars left in Britain to hunt, so Christmas dinner became a goose.

• In Tudor times William Strickland sailed the Atlantic and brought back turkeys to Britain. In 1550 William's coat of arms was updated to show a turkey. (Imagine riding into battle with a turkey on your shield? The enemy would die laughing.)

• King James I (born 1566 – died 1625) didn't much like boar's head. So he was one of the first to feast on turkey at Christmas.

• Turkeys were rare for another couple of hundred years until the 1700s when King George II got a taste for eating the bird. He fenced off part of Richmond Park in London to breed them.

• In the 1800s, when Queen Victoria was on the throne, turkey became more popular than goose for Christmas and it still is. Queen Victoria's colossal Christmas feasts meant the chop for 50 turkeys. (She did have nine children but that's still a lot of bird meat.)

27 DECEMBER
On this horrible day in history …

1836

You see a lot of snow on Christmas cards, they're covered in sweet snowmen and snowy sleighs. You hear people on the radio singing that classic song … what's it called? Oh, 'I Wish I Could Be Dreaming of a White Christmas in a Winter Wonderland with Frosty the Snowman Every Day' – that's it!

But snow can be a horribly cold killer. Ask Scott of the Antarctic … oh, sorry, you can't. The snow killed him. Never mind, read the old newspapers of Lewes in Sussex instead. On this day in 1836 there is a disaster and it's snow joke. Snow falls in the South of England in drifts up to 12 metres deep.

The town of Lewes stands in the shadow of a cliff a hundred metres high. That winter the snow gathers in a frozen mountain on top of the cliff. The people are told to move out for safety. They say, 'We're not scared of a bit of snow.' On 27 December the sun shines and the mountain of snow cracks.

The big white slide at Lewes

When the snow collapses it falls on Boulder Row below, wiping out a row of cottages and killing eight people. Seven survive. It is the worst avalanche ever known in Britain.

A pub is built on the site. The rather cruel owner calls it 'The Snowdrop Inn'.

SNOW. DROP ... GEDDIT? I THINK THAT IS FUNNY. HORRIBLE ... BUT FUNNY.

28
DECEMBER

ON THE FOURTH DAY OF CHRISTMAS,
THE RATTUS SENT TO ME...
FOUR WORKHOUSE PAUPERS,
THREE ROASTED DORMICE,
TWO BOMBS A-DROPPED,
AND A HORR-I-BLE HIS-TOR-EE.

WORKHOUSE WOE

YOU WOULD NOT WANT TO GO TO THE WORKHOUSE FOR CHRISTMAS ... OR AT ANY OTHER TIME FOR THAT MATTER. IF YOU WERE STARVING AND HAD NO JOB THEN YOU WOULD BE LET IN TO YOUR NEAREST WORKHOUSE, BUT THEY WERE COLD AND CHEERLESS PLACES WITH THE FOULEST FOOD AND ITCHY, FLEA-FILLED BEDS.

47

By the 1830s most towns and villages had at least one workhouse. In 1797 Sir Frederick Eden wrote:

"The workhouse is an awful building, with small windows, low rooms and dark staircases. It has a high wall, that makes it look like a prison, and keeps out fresh air. There are 8 or 10 beds in each room, made from old wool that hold in all scents and are home to all vermin. The passages all need whitewashing. No one counts births and deaths, but when smallpox, measles or fevers appear in the house, the deaths are very great. Of 131 people in the house, 60 are children."

The young hero of Charles Dickens's famous book *Oliver Twist* spent some time in a workhouse. When he asked for more food he was punished.

In Victorian England workhouse life really was hard and the places were hated. Rioters burned down a workhouse in Narberth in 1839. In Carmarthen a girl called Frances Evans led the poor people to wreck their workhouse. Soldiers rode in to beat them down. The poor wanted "Better food, free tools and freedom." Not a lot to ask for, is it?

The work was hard. Bone-crushing was a job the poor were often forced to do. But in the Andover workhouse in 1845 an inspector found that starving people ended up fighting over the bones to suck out the marrow or scrape off the scraps of rotten meat.

People fit to work were allowed to stay in their homes and given money to help them – it was called 'outdoor relief.' But in 1844 that was stopped. If you were poor and starving you had no choice but to enter the workhouse or die.

Christmas in the workhouse was not much fun, as you might expect. The rich people would come and eat Christmas dinner with the poor. They were trying to show how much they cared. A famous poem was written telling the sad tale of a man who begged for outdoor relief for his sick wife at Christmas. He was refused and his wife died. The poem tells the story of his sitting at the Christmas workhouse dinner and telling the rich how his wife was refused outdoor relief and died. Here is a cut-down version of the poignant poem:

Christmas Day
In the Workhouse

It is Christmas Day in the
Workhouse,
And the cold bare walls are bright
With garlands of green and holly,
And the place is a pleasant sight:

And the guardians and their ladies,
Although the wind is east,
Have come in their furs and wrappers,
To watch their charges feast;

But one of the old men mutters,
And pushes his plate aside:
'Great God!' he cries; 'but it
chokes me!
For this is the day she died.'

The guardians gazed in horror,
The master's face went white;
'Did a pauper refuse the pudding?'
Could their ears believe aright?

But the pauper looked at the ladies,
Then, eyeing their lords, he said,
'I eat not the food of villains
Whose hands are foul and red:

'Last winter my wife lay dying,
Starved in a filthy den;
I had never been to the workhouse,
I came to the workhouse then.

And what do you think they told me,
Mocking my awful grief?
That 'the House' was open to us,
But they wouldn't give 'out relief.'

They drove me away with curses;
Then I fought with a dog in the street,
And tore from the mongrel's clutches
A crust he was trying to eat.

'There, get ye gone to your
dinners;
Don't mind me in the least;
Think of the happy paupers
Eating your Christmas feast.'

George Robert Sims (1847 – 1922)

Yes, there, in a land of plenty,
Lay a loving woman dead,
Cruelly starved and murdered
For a loaf of the parish bread.

Tragic, huh? This gloomy tale was often parodied, with silly alternative versions being performed in comedy shows and vaudeville theatres. Versions a bit like this one:

It was Christmas in the workhouse
The snow was raining fast
A bare-footed man with clogs on
Came slowly whizzing past
He turned around a straight crooked corner
To see a dead donkey die
He pulled out his gun to stab him
The donkey spat in his eye

28 DECEMBER
On this horrible day in history …

1879

A terrific storm hits Scotland and damages the railway bridge over the River Tay. The engine driver doesn't see this and drives across in the stormy dark. The train topples off the bridge into the icy waters below. All 75 people on board are killed, of course.

The bridge has been open for just 18 months and the man paid to look after the iron girders is Henry Noble.

Henry is a brick-layer by trade, so he doesn't spot the wobbles in the iron girders.

Some people in England say it serves the passengers right – they should not have been travelling on a Sunday, a day when they should have been in church.

The day after the disaster, hundreds of people go to the river bank to stare at the broken bridge and watch divers searching for bodies. Even today ghouls go to gawp at scenes of catastrophes.

To make the disaster even more tragic the poet William Topaz McGonagall (1825 – 1902) wrote one of the worst poems EVER.

Here are a couple of verses … if you can bear to read them …

'Beautiful Railway Bridge of the Silvery Tay!
Alas! I am very sorry to say
That ninety lives have been taken away
On the last Sabbath day of 1879,
Which will be remember'd for a very long time.

'Your central girders would not have given way,
At least many sensible men do say,
Had they been supported on each side with buttresses,
At least many sensible men confesses,
For the stronger we our houses do build,
The less chance we have of being killed.'

Only 36 bodies were found and buried, but divers DID find the locomotive. It was hauled out, repaired and went on running for another 40 years. The railway workers called the cursed loco 'The Diver'.

That's a horrible joke if ever I heard one.[6]

6. Read more gruesome tales of Scotland in *Horrible Histories Scotland*.

29
DECEMBER

ON THE FIFTH DAY OF CHRISTMAS,
THE RATTUS SENT TO ME...
FIVE ASSASSINS,
FOUR WORKHOUSE PAUPERS,
THREE ROASTED DORMICE,
TWO BOMBS A-DROPPED,
AND A HORR-I-BLE HIS-TOR-EE.

AWFUL FOR ANIMALS

CHRISTMAS IS A TIME OF REINDEER AND ROBINS ... AND RATS OF COURSE. ALL THAT FOOD THROWN IN THE BINS FOR US RODENTS TO CHOMP AND CHEW — DELICIOUS! YES, CHRISTMAS CAN BE A FINE TIME FOR SOME ANIMALS, BUT FOR OTHERS IT IS NOT ALWAYS SO HORRIBLY HAPPY...

Big fat lemming lies

There is a creature that is smaller than a rat but just as furry. It lives near the Arctic. Father Christmas probably has them in the forests outside his front door. But you wouldn't believe the lemming lies that are told about Rattus's cold cousins.

LEMMING LIE 1

In the 1530s, during the age of the Terrible Tudors, there was a man called Zeigler of Strasbourg. He wrote books about strange creatures. He said lemmings were born in the clouds and fell down to earth like apples off a tree when the winds blew.

LEMMING LIE 2

Then along came a scientist called Ole Worm (who lived in Denmark from 1588 – 1655) – honestly I didn't make that name up, or that of his father Willum Worm. Anyway, Ole Worm said Zeigler was talking nonsense. Ole said that lemmings DID fall from the sky, but they were swept up from the earth by whirlwinds. The flying lemmings were carried on the wind and dropped from the sky when the storm died down.

LEMMING LIE 3

Lemmings really do sometimes set off in a pack to hunt for new feeding places. When they come to a river they swim across it, and some of them drown – *awww*. People started to think the lemmings threw themselves into those icy rivers to kill themselves. (Some people cross the road and get killed by cars ... that doesn't mean people cross the road because they want to kill themselves.) The story of lemmings drowning themselves is a loathsome lie.

THAT'S CHEATING

LEMMING LIE 4

In 1958 the Walt Disney film company made a movie that seemed to show lemmings leaping to their deaths off a cliff in Norway. Then the whole world believed that lemmings drowned themselves. But the film was a big fat fake. The lemmings on the film were from Hudson Bay (in Canada) and they were flown to a cliff in Calgary in Canada (not Norway, no-way.) They were put on a turntable and when it started to spin they were thrown over the edge of the cliff.

Reindeer runners

Reindeer are funny creatures, but they're as Christmassy as they come. Here are some big fat facts to amaze your friends about Rudolph and company.

1 In the old myths of northern Europe, Thor was the god of thunder. He rode across the skies in a cart pulled by two goats, but this ancient tale may be where the story of Santa's flying sleigh came from. The goats were fierce creatures called Snarler and Teeth Grinder.

It may sound a jolly job for a goat – a bit like Rudolph flying around with Santa – but it was not all that much fun for Snarler and Teeth Grinder. Every day Thor would eat them for his dinner. The next day he'd bring them back to life, as fresh as newly stuffed sausages, flying across the sky. One day he shared the goat meat with a family of peasants. A child snapped open a bone to suck out the marrow. The goat came back to life the next morning, but with a broken leg.

At least Rudolph didn't get eaten by Santa. If he did we'd be singing, "Rudolph the red-nosed reindeer, had a very chewy nose."

2 Travelling tribesmen called the Sami knew that 'fly agaric' toadstools would give them fantastic dreams. But those mushrooms are poisonous to humans. The Sami fed the mushrooms to their reindeer. The reindeer's guts removed the poisons but left the dreamy drug, which came out in the reindeer pee. All the tribesmen had to do was drink the pee, and they would have dreams about all sorts of fantastical things … like flying reindeer.

3 In 1823 Clement Clarke Moore wrote the famous poem, 'A Visit from St Nicholas' and it is all about Santa and his flying reindeer. Here's just a taster:

"...The moon on the breast of the new-fallen snow,

Gave a lustre of midday to objects below,

When what to my wondering eyes did appear,

But a miniature sleigh and eight tiny rein-deer,

With a little old driver so lively and quick,

I knew in a moment he must be St Nick.

More rapid than eagles his coursers they came,

And he whistled, and shouted, and called them by name:

"Now, Dasher! now, Dancer! now Prancer and Vixen!

On, Comet! on, Cupid! on, Donder and Blitzen!

To the top of the porch! to the top of the wall!

Now dash away! dash away! dash away all!"

As leaves that before the wild hurricane fly,

When they meet with an obstacle, mount to the sky;

So up to the housetop the coursers they flew

With the sleigh full of toys, and St Nicholas too…

And then, in a twinkling, I heard on the roof

The prancing and pawing of each little hoof …"

Someone asked Clement if Santa's reindeer were boys or girls. Before he could explain this, a woman said that they were female. Clement asked her how she was so sure, she replied, 'That silly St Nicholas man would get lost if he didn't have girls to guide him, wouldn't he?'

Deadly donkeys

THE BIBLE SAYS A DONKEY CARRIED MARY TO BETHLEHEM WHERE JESUS WAS BORN. THE DONKEY WAS THERE ON THE FIRST CHRISTMAS NIGHT, SO THE ANIMAL BECAME A HOLY SORT OF CREATURE AT CHRISTMAS.

TEN DONKEY BELIEFS

1 Donkeys have a cross of dark hair on their backs, on the spot where Mary sat as she was carried to Bethlehem to give birth to Jesus. People believe this cross is the mark of God.

2 People also believe that donkey cross has the magical power to cure all sorts of problems – from toothache to fits.

3 Passing a child three times under and over a donkey is supposed to cure whooping cough.

4 Sometimes donkey hairs were mixed with bread and eaten for luck. Tasty hair burger eh?

5 Sometimes you would have to put a sick person's hair in the donkey's food for it to eat. The illness would be cured.

6 In the fifth century a poet, Aurelius Clemens, said that the donkeys and other animals in the stable where Jesus was born could speak. He said it was so they could join the angels in praising the baby Jesus.

7 In 1223, the Pope allowed St Francis of Assisi to use live animals, including a donkey, on stage to tell the Christmas story in a play. These 'Nativity' plays became popular around the world.

8 The nativity stories added the tale of Aurelius Clemens and the talking animals. The plays showed that God had given animals in the stable the power to speak for an hour at midnight on Christmas Eve.

9 But beware ... it's very bad luck to catch the animals chatting. One thing you may hear is the donkeys debating whether their master will die before the next Christmas. If YOU own the donkey that is NOT something you want to know.

10 In Britain the story has been changed. The animals in British legends never do their Christmas chatting when there is a human around to hear.

Rocking robins

BIG FAT ROBINS ARE BOBBIN' ALL OVER CHRISTMAS CARDS. WHY DON'T WE SEE SEAGULLS OR SPARROWS, BLUEBIRDS OR BUDGIES? WHAT'S SO SPECIAL ABOUT ROBINS?

Merry Christmas

• Robins like to be nosey ... oh all right, they don't have noses just beaks, so I suppose we have to call them beaky. Anyway, they hang around humans so people think they are being 'friendly'.

• There are Christian legends about how the robin got its red breast. When Jesus was crucified He was given a crown of thorns. The story goes that a robin tried to pluck a thorn from Jesus's head and spiked its own breast. The red is blood. Cheerful eh?

• Another legend tells us that a little brown robin was actually having a snooze in the rafters of the stable that Jesus was born in. When the wise men came with their gifts, the little robin woke up and realised that this was no ordinary baby. He kept watch over the family as night fell, and when the fire began to go out he flew down and flapped his wings over the embers to get the flames going again. In the process, he burnt his chest feathers, and they turned a glowing red. Poor old robin.

• Robins are definitely seen as helpful little birds. Early Christian mythology sees a robin rescuing St Leonorius, a sixth-century Welsh missionary. St Leonorius and his monks set up a new monastery in Brittany then realized they had no seeds to plant wheat to feed themselves. (How stupid were they?) Along came a robin with a head of corn in its beak and gave them enough seed to start their farm. They wouldn't get much bread from a single head of corn but they did … it was a miracle. Another story says the robin flitted along the road and led them to a store of wheat. It must have been some other farmer's wheat, so I guess they were robin it …

FOR A MONK THAT'S A BAD HABIT … MONKS WEAR ROBES CALLED HABITS. BAD HABIT … GET IT? OH, NEVER MIND.

• In the 1800s there were poets writing tales of robins. A children's rhyming picture book tells the horrible tale of the Babes in the Wood – the story of two orphan children who were left in the woods to die by their wicked uncle. The little robin was too late to save their lives, but he covered their bodies with leaves as a form of burial.

• A story is told of a monkish miracle. The monk was a boy at the time and grew up to be Saint Kentigern. His sobbin' robin story is told on the next page …

KENTIGERN AND THE DEAD
RED ROBIN

ONCE upon a time an old saint called Servan kept a monastery school near Glasgow in Scotland. Kentigern was one of the smallest boys but the cleverest at reading, writing and singing. Saint Servan loved him best of all his pupils. Many of the boys hated smarty-pants Kentigern, and you can see why.

The boys planned a trap to make Kentigern look wicked. They all had to take turns in keeping the monastery fire alight. When it was Kentigern's turn some boys led him away while others put out the fire. Disaster. But Kentigern blew on the cold ashes, set the fire going again and was saved. A miracle.

The boys hated him more than a cold bath now. They needed another plot — a really cruel and evil one this time. Their master, Saint Servan, had a robin redbreast as a pet. It would eat its breakfast from his hand. (Let's hope the little redbreast didn't perch on his bowl and poop in his porridge, eh?) The robin would sing along with the hymns.

Now, one morning, the boys killed the little redbreast and pulled off his head. (It wouldn't be singing many hymns after that.)

One of the killer kids ran to Saint Servan. 'Oh Father, look what the wicked Kentigern has done. He's ripped off robin's nut.'

Saint Servan took the little body in his hand and went to look for Kentigern. 'Look at this, boy,' he cried. 'What shall I do to punish the robin-ripper?'

Kentigern asked, 'Who has killed him, Father?'

'You did, you did. We saw you,' cried all the bad boys.

'I did not do it, Father.'

'Can you prove it?' asked Saint Servan.

'Give me the robin, Father,' said Kentigern, then holding the limp body in one hand and the head in the other, he looked up towards heaven, and said a little prayer.

Then he set the head in place where it should be and, as his tears fell upon the robin's neck. The feathers ruffled and the little wings fluttered; the black eyes opened, and it gave a little chirp.

Then the robin hopped out of Kentigern's hand and flew up on his master's shoulder. There he sat and sang a beautiful hymn of joy.

The bad boys were punished and Kentigern and the robin became the best of friends ... until they both died of old age of course. They were buried and lived happily ever under.

29 DECEMBER
On this horrible day in history …

In 1170 Thomas Becket was King Henry II's best mate. The king made Tom the head of the Church – the Archbishop of Canterbury.

Henry   **Tom**

Tom and Henry quarrelled and one Christmas evening the king complained that he wished he was rid of his old pal. Some knights were at the dinner table and thought Henry II really meant it. They set off to find Tom and give him the chop.

On 29 December the knights find the archbishop in Canterbury Cathedral. They wouldn't kill him in such a holy place, would they? Oh yes they would. They take out their swords and slice and dice Becket to death as he clutches at his altar.

When the king gets the news of Archbishop Tom's slaying he is shocked and sorry to the jewelled tips of his fingers and the booted tips of his toes… a bit late then, of course. Henry says he never meant it and feels it is all his fault … which it is.

To punish himself, the king goes to the scene of the murder, walking barefoot into the cathedral and praying. There are several monks and priests there. How do they complete the punishment of the king? They strip him to the waist and take it in turn to give him three to five lashes each.

(That's more lashes than you have on your eyes!)[7]

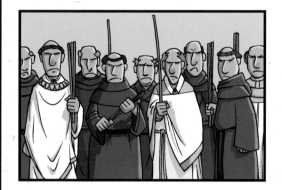

7. Read more about Becket and the wars of the Middle Ages in *Horrible Histories Measly Middle Ages.*

30
DECEMBER

ON THE SIXTH DAY OF CHRISTMAS,
THE RATTUS SENT TO ME ...
SIX SNOWY STORMS,
FIVE ASSASSINS,
FOUR WORKHOUSE PAUPERS,
THREE ROASTED DORMICE,
TWO BOMBS A-DROPPED,
AND A HORR-I-BLE HIS-TOR-EE.

WILD WEATHER

THE TWELVE NIGHTS OF CHRISTMAS OFTEN SEE WOEFUL WINTER WEATHER THAT BRINGS TEMPESTS TO TOWNS, HURRICANES TO HOUSES, SNOWSTORMS TO CITIES AND GALES TO GARDENS. WINDS THAT WHIP WILD WAVES AT SEA BRING WRECKS AND RUIN TO STRUGGLING SHIPS.

I'M COLD

Christmas cheer isn't enough to stop the weather from being truly horrible, and if things get bad on land, they're often even worse out at sea. On Christmas Day 1951 the *SS Flying Enterprise* was hit by a monster wave and started to crack up. That's happened to lots of forgotten ships of course, but this one was remembered because the battered ship was filmed from an aeroplane and the film was shown on television.

The world watched the amazing story of Captain Henrik Carlsen who saw everyone on board rescued but said, 'I will not leave my ship.' Tugs tried to tow *Flying Enterprise* to port through the howling gales but the ropes snapped and the ship sank in the sea. Captain Carlsen was the last man to leave before she sank under the waves.

It's not just the ships that are in danger though. Lighthouse keepers are the brave blokes out there who sit alone high up in tall towers keeping brilliant bulbs blinking to steer ships away from razor rocks. They have saved countless lives, but one December night in 1900 it was the keepers who suffered in one of the spookiest Christmas-time history mysteries of all.

FEAR ON FLANNAN ISLES

Three lighthouse keepers seem to have vanished from the face of the earth. Lighthouse inspector Robert Muirhead visited the island today looking for answers - and looking for the three missing men. He found no answers. No men.

'I know they were there on 15 December,' he told our reporter. 'The lighthouse light went out on 15 December. We know that. But a ship couldn't get to the island until Boxing Day to see what was wrong.'

What did the crew of the Boxing Day ship find? 'There was no flag on the flagpole,' Muirhead reported, 'no food boxes waiting to be filled and no lighthouse keepers rowing out to meet the boat,' he explained.

Joe Moore rowed ashore and went to the keepers' house to find out where they were. The doors were all locked, their beds had been slept in and the clock had stopped. There had been a set of oilskin coats to shelter the men from the worst of the weather. There was just one coat there. Muirhead said, 'It looks as if one man had gone out without a coat. In the December storms he must have been crazy to go out without a coat.'

Joe Moore found the lighthouse lamps were cleaned and filled with oil, ready to light. A chair in the kitchen had been knocked over. The man searched the island and there was not another person to be found.

He reported back to the ship and the captain sent a message to the mainland: 'Poor fellows must have been blown over the cliffs or drowned or something like that.'

Mr Muirhead said, 'There was terrible damage on the landing stage. The storm had ripped and twisted iron railings, washed away a store-house and thrown huge crates around. I believe the men went to try and rescue the crates but were washed away by a mammoth wave.'

That sounds sensible but people in the Oban Inn have their own ideas about what happened.

Mrs Kilwellie from the Post Office said, 'My Archie says one keeper murdered the other two and felt so guilty he threw himself into the sea.'

Her neighbour, Mrs McKay, argued, 'We've heard about the monster of Loch Ness. Well there are bigger monsters out at sea. It was a monster carried them off.'

'Or a huge bird,' her husband said.

'The men were missing their women,' Ellen Bruce said. 'When they saw a mermaid they ran into the sea to catch her and she drowned them. That's what mermaids do for sport.'

'Nonsense and fairy tales,'

the inn-keeper said. 'There are German spies all around. The keepers saw a German warship off the coast, doing things it shouldn't. The Germans landed and shot them to keep them quiet.'

The Oban police sergeant, Peter Blackwell, scoffed at these ideas. 'Everyone has heard ghost stories of the Flannan Phantom. Take my word for it, an evil spirit made the men terrified. There was nowhere to run so they threw themselves off the cliffs.'

Inspector Robert Muirhead said, 'The fact is we may never know the truth.'

But so long as no one knows what happened the people of the Hebrides will walk the shores in fear of monsters and ghosts, birds and waves.

The Christmas mystery has never been solved. Some people think the keepers were snatched by aliens from outer space. There have been songs and poems and books about the mystery. There has even been an episode of *Doctor Who* about it. A poet called Wilfrid Gibson wrote as if he was one of the men who landed and found an empty island …

Yet, as we crowded through the door,
We only saw a table spread
For dinner, meat, and cheese and bread;
But, all untouched; and no-one there,
As though, when they sat down to eat,
'Ere they could even taste,
Alarm had come, and they in haste
Had risen and left the bread and meat,
For at the table head a chair
Lay tumbled on the floor.

Spooky … but wrong. There was NO meal on the table. Someone had tidied the kitchen up before disaster struck. Maybe it was a very tidy little green man from Mars. Did he cry to his little green friends, 'Take the humans to the flying saucer … I'll just do the washing up before we leave. Now where did I put me rubber gloves?'

I don't think so. It was probably Rattus.

It's not just history that has seen horrible weather. On 24 December 2013 gale-force winds and heavy rain hit Britain. Rivers flooded and people drowned, electric pylons snapped and left people with no light or cooking for their Christmas turkeys. In the USA it was even worse. The storm at Christmas 2013 brought freezing cold, heavy snow, ice, flooding, rain, fog, winds of 75 miles an hour, terrible thunderstorms and tornadoes. Bah, humbug!

30 DECEMBER
On this horrible day in history ...

1460

The Battle of Wakefield takes place on this day. You probably know the rhyme:

The Grand old Duke of York
He had ten thousand men.
He marched them up to the
top of the hill
Then he marched them
down again.

This is the battle where the Grand Old Duke of York dies. His army is fighting against King Henry VI. They arrive in icy Wakefield and the Duke marches them up the hill into Sandal Castle. (There are 6,000 men, not 10,000 by the way.) They spend a chilly Christmas there.

The king's men surround them. They will wait for the Grand Old Duke's men to starve.

The Duke's men are cold and hungry and crowded inside the little castle walls. On 30 December they see the king's men in the valley below. It looks like a small army. The Duke and his men decide to charge down,

break out of their castle trap and escape to safety.

But the king's troops are hiding in the woods. Once the Grand Old Duke is down the hill they come out and kill him. Even the Duke's 17-year-old son is killed in cold blood, begging for his life.

The Duke's head is cut off and stuck on a pole over the gateway to the City of York. The rotting head is given a paper crown – as if to say, 'You wanted the king's crown? Here's one we made earlier. Ho-ho-ho.'

31
DECEMBER

ON THE SEVENTH DAY OF CHRISTMAS,
THE RATTUS SENT TO ME ...
SEVEN SPOOKY STORIES, SIX SNOWY STORMS,
FIVE ASSASSINS, FOUR WORKHOUSE PAUPERS,
THREE ROASTED DORMICE,
TWO BOMBS A-DROPPED,
AND A HORR-I-BLE HIS-TOR-EE.

SPOOKS AND SPIRITS

CHARLES DICKENS WAS A WRITER IN THE DAYS OF QUEEN VICTORIA. HE WROTE THE FAMOUS STORY, *A CHRISTMAS CAROL* ABOUT MR SCROOGE AND THE GHOSTS OF CHRISTMAS. IT WAS SO POPULAR THAT HE STARTED WRITING A NEW CHRISTMAS STORY EVERY YEAR.

Goblins and ghouls

Here's Dickens's story from 1844; it's called *The Chimes* and is about a goblin. This is a version of Mr Dickens's tale that Rattus has helpfully rewritten to make shorter...

THE STORY OF
'THE CHIMES'

It's New Year's Eve and Trotty, the old messenger, is miserable. The world is such a cruel and crime-filled place. His daughter Meg is planning to marry Richard the next day but they are so very poor it only makes Trotty more unhappy.

He goes to bed and is woken by the sound of bells. Ring, ring and ding-a-ling. They are calling for him. 'Trot-come, Trot-come, Trot, Trot, Trot come.' You can't sleep with a row like that going on can you?

Dickens says "For the night-wind has a dismal trick of wandering round a building of that sort, and moaning as it goes ... it wails and howls ... and creeps along the walls, seeming to read, in whispers, the Inscriptions sacred to the Dead. At some of these, it moans and cries as if it were lamenting. It has a ghostly sound."

So off Trotty trotted to see what they wanted. Through the cold, cobbled streets Trotty tottered till he came to the bell tower of the church. The tower door was open (which is just as well or there would be no story.) He went into the dark stairway and climbed the winding spiral stairs. Ring, ring and ding-a-ling. Trot-come, Trot-come, Trot, Trot, Trot come.'

It was driving him crazy … it's driving *me* crazy. When he reached the top he found the spooky spirit of the bells waiting for him. And there is the spirit servant, a goblin. 'It's New Year, you miserable old goat,' the goblin cries. 'Things can only get better.'

'Poppycock, balderdash and gargoyles,' Trotty scoffs.

'You think things are wretched now? Let me show you just how miserable they can get,' the goblin says. 'Let me show you the future.'

'How can I see into the future?' Trotty asks. 'No human can do that.'

'Ah but you're not a human, you're a ghost,' the goblin giggles. 'You fell off this here church tower and killed yourself. Now look at the grim future for those you've left behind.'

Trotty seems to stare through the walls of the tower and down to the town below.

Dickens says "Stone, and brick, and slate, and tile, became transparent to him as to them. He saw the goblin and the spirit of the bells in the houses, busy at the sleepers' beds. He saw them soothing people in their dreams; he saw them beating them with knotted whips; he saw them yelling in their ears; he saw them playing softest music on their pillows; he saw them cheering some with the songs of birds and the perfume of flowers; he saw them flashing awful faces on the troubled rest of others, from enchanted mirrors which they carried in their hands."

The goblin points. 'See, there's Richard … he is ruined by

drink. Meg marries him but she can't save him. He dies –
and leaves poor Meg with their baby and no money.'

'Poor Meg,' Trotty sighs.

'Don't worry,' the goblin grins. 'She has the answer. She can
throw herself and the baby off the bridge and kill them both.
See? She's on the bridge now. She's tottering, Trotty.'

'No … save her,' the old man moans and stretches out a hand,
through the walls of the tower, over the roofs and gardens of
the town, past the shops and over the cobbled roads. (You can
do that when you're a ghost.) He clutches at Meg's arm and
pulls her back from the brink.

'I was wrong,' Trotty tells the goblin. 'If this is the future
it's much worse than the life I had. I wish I could go back and
stop all that happening.'

'But you can,' the goblin shrugs. He vanishes. Trotty blinks.
And when he opens his eyes he finds he is in his bed and the
spirit of the bells was all a dream.

The bells are ringing again. Ring, ring and ding-a-ling. They
are calling for him. 'Trot-come, Trot-come, Trot, Trot, Trot
come.' But this time they are wedding bells ringing for Meg
and Richard's wedding day.

And if they don't live happily ever after then I'm a goblin.

Charles Dickens is one of the greatest writers in the world – ever. But, as you can see, he uses the worst story-ending in the world – ever: 'He woke up and it had all been a dream.' Oh dear.

Teacher tale

Dickens's 1848 story, *The Haunted Man* has a better ending ... just no gruesome goblins.

Redlaw is a chemistry teacher and an angry man who is haunted by a ghost that looks just like himself. The teacher is as ugly as a ghost to begin with ...

Everyone could see his hollow cheek; his sunken brilliant eye; his black-suited figure, indefinably grim, his grizzled hair hanging, like tangled sea-weed, about his face.

(Reminds me of my teacher ... she was scary.)

This spook tells Redlaw that he can allow him to forget everything unhappy that has ever happened to him ... and chemistry teachers have a lot to be unhappy about.

Redlaw agrees. The spirit vanishes, and Redlaw forgets the bad times ... but he becomes angrier than ever. Only a young lady named Milly can calm him down. She tells him we all NEED to remember the bad times – that way we may learn to forgive and forget.

Redlaw, like Ebenezer Scrooge, is a changed, more loving person, who learns to be humble at Christmas.

Story superstar

Dickens's most famous Christmas story – *A Christmas Carol* – was so popular he went around Britain and America telling the story on stage. It's a little long so he made it shorter and told it in 90 minutes ... the same as a football match but without a ball.

Dickens was so famous that when he died in 1870 a little market girl in London gasped ...

Mr Dickens dead? Then will Father Christmas die too? [8]

8. Read more about the world of Dickens and Queen Victoria in *Horrible Histories Villainous Victorians*.

Stage scare

In 1862 an inventor called John Henry 'Professor' Pepper decided to turn Dickens's *The Haunted Man* into a scary stage play for Christmas. He came up with a clever trick to make a ghost 'appear' on stage.

He used lights and mirrors to make an actor appear on a sheet of glass. The people in the theatre could see through the actor's image just as you could through a phantom. The trick is known as 'Pepper's Ghost' and it's still used around the world in places like museums and on ghost trains at theme parks to terrify visitors.

Christmas crackers don't tell good ghost jokes. But they tell lots of very bad ghost jokes …

Q. What do witches use in their hair?
A. Scare-spray

Q. Who was the most famous ghost detective?
A. Sherlock Moans

Q. What kind of roads do ghosts haunt?
A. Dead ends!

Q. What is a ghost's favourite game?
A. Hide-and-SHRIEK

Sovereign spooks

Some castles and old royal houses are said to be haunted by so many ghosts that they could have their own festive phantom parties together at Christmas. I bet they have a *waaaaail* of a time!

• Queen Elizabeth, the present Queen's mother, came from one of Britain's most haunted castles, Glamis in Scotland.

There are the ghosts of . . .

the cruel Earl Beardie who haunts his old rooms

a tongueless woman

a lady in white

a little black boy

the Grey Lady – said to be Lady Glamis who was buried alive and seen by the Queen Mother herself.

• Anne Boleyn was beheaded by her husband Henry VIII. It must be hard for her to find her way around without a head. Her ghost is seen all over the place.

She is said to haunt :

The Tower of London (where she was executed)

Hampton Court Palace (where she lived with Henry)

Blickling Hall in Norfolk (where she lived before her marriage)

King's Manor in York (where she has a ghostly monk for company)

At least her ghost isn't lonely. Each of those places has several other ghosts who live there.

• Edward II was murdered in Berkeley Castle. For centuries afterwards his ghostly screams could still be heard at night.

• If you want to meet a sovereign spook then go to Farnham in Surrey. There you can meet . . .

Henry VIII

Mary I

Elizabeth I

James I

George III

Victoria

• Elizabeth II's country home at Sandringham is haunted at Christmas. Each Christmas Eve the Christmas cards are thrown to the floor. (Of course it could simply be a very draughty old house.)[9]

9. If you want to read more about Britain's peculiar monarchs look at *Horrible Histories Cruel Kings and Mean Queens.*

31 DECEMBER
On this horrible day in history ...

AD 192

The Romans had some dangerous emperors but Commodus was one of the worst. He became emperor when he was just 15 years old. It is said he ...

... killed five hippopotami in a day with his bare hands.

... had a hundred bears put in an arena then fired spears and arrows from a safe platform until he'd killed them all.

... beheaded ostriches in an arena with sickle-headed arrows.

… gathered all the men in the city who had lost their feet from disease or accident. He killed them with blows from a club, pretending they were giants.

… had a wife and a sister executed as well as his most faithful servant.

On New Year's Eve he makes a daft mistake. He writes a list of people he wants to execute. At the top of the list is his girlfriend, Marcia. But Marcia finds the list. She decides to kill the emperor before he can kill her.

She gives him poisoned wine … but it only makes him sick. Then she pays a young athlete to strangle Commodus.

He dies before he can wish anyone Happy New Year. He is aged just 31.

A year later, Marcia is executed for killing Commodus. Roman days can be rotten.

1
JANUARY

**ON THE EIGHTH DAY OF CHRISTMAS,
THE RATTUS SENT TO ME ...**
EIGHT SLAUGHTERED SOLDIERS,
SEVEN SPOOKY STORIES, SIX SNOWY STORMS,
FIVE ASSASSINS, FOUR WORKHOUSE PAUPERS,
THREE ROASTED DORMICE,
TWO BOMBS A-DROPPED,
AND A HORR-I-BLE HIS-TOR-EE.

GORE AND GAMES

CHRISTMAS IS A TIME FOR GAMES, AND PLAYING A GAME TO WIN IS A GREAT WAY TO START A FIGHT. BUT THERE WAS ONE GAME THAT BROUGHT PEACE AT CHRISTMAS WHEN ALL AROUND WAS WAR, BLOOD AND FROZEN MUD.

THAT GAME HAPPENED IN 1914. THE FIRST WORLD WAR HAD BROKEN OUT. THE BRITISH TROOPS HAD BEEN STANDING IN THEIR ICY TRENCHES WITH RATS LIKE ME FOR COMPANY WHILE THEY SHOT AT THEIR GERMAN ENEMIES WITH BULLETS AND SHELLS. THEN CHRISTMAS MORNING DAWNED AND SOMETHING VERY STRANGE HAPPENED. PEACE BROKE OUT ...

Here is the true tale told in a radio play … record it with your friends if you like. It needs three people, but George can also play the part of Heinrich if there are just two of you.

The Christmas Truce

CAST:

<u>Tommy:</u> Young British soldier from Yorkshire. A little scared.

<u>George:</u> Old British soldier. Tired and bored.

<u>Heinrich:</u> German soldier. Young and serious.

<u>SCENE</u> — In a British Trench in France

<u>Tommy:</u> (Tells the story) It was Christmas Day, 1914 in the trenches. We were supposed to be shooting at the German enemy a hundred yards away. But it was scary. If you looked over the top of the trench THEY would shoot at YOU. And it was cold. The trenches were usually full of mud, but even the mud had frozen hard. Then, on Christmas Night, the shooting stopped. I turned to my old friend George.

Tommy: It's quiet, isn't it George?

George: It's Christmas, young Tommy. It's a truce. We won't bother Jerry and he won't bother us. So you just enjoy your Christmas.

Tommy: I've got me chocolate and me tobacco and me Christmas card from the King and Queen! It's in His Majesty's own handwriting too. It says, 'May God protect you and bring you home safe.'

George: Here, what's that noise?

Tommy: Sounds like a brass band. What's a brass band doing in the middle of a war? Have a look, George.

George: Have a look? Have a LOOK? And get me brains blown out?

Tommy: No, listen. The Germans are playing Christmas carols!

Heinrich: (Singing *Silent Night* in German) 'Stille Nacht, Heilige Nacht …'

Tommy: (Telling the story) So I raised my head above the edge. Nobody fired. And I saw a wonderful sight. The Germans had put up little Christmas trees with candles. I shouted across to them, a bit cheeky …

Tommy: (Calls out) Happy Christmas, Jerry!

Heinrich: Happy Christmas, Tommy!

Tommy: (To George) See? They're friendly!

Heinrich: (Shouts back) Come here, Tommy. Shake hands. You don't shoot. We don't shoot.

Tommy: (Telling story) George tried to stop me but a lot of the lads left the trenches and met the Germans in the bit between the trenches — the muddy patch we called No-man's Land. Then someone found a football.

Heinrich: I think maybe we have a game. We Germans play against you British?

Tommy: You're on. I'm good at football.

Tommy: (Telling story) So we marked out a pitch, right there in No-man's Land. I got picked as right winger. For an hour there were no war – but there were plenty of conflict! Every time I ran forward I were tripped by this big German.

Heinrich: Five minutes to go and you are losing one-nil. Hah! We beat you British.

Tommy: That made me a bit mad. I got the ball and ran to their goal. I saw the big German charging towards me! He skidded over the frozen mud in a slide that would have broken my ankle. I jumped over his legs and ran on. The goalkeeper dived too soon. I waited and slid the ball between the goalposts!
(There is a whistle)

Heinrich: Ah, full time. A draw. One-one.

Tommy: (Telling story)   When I turned round the German was standing there.

Heinrich: Shake hand, Englishman. Well played.

Tommy: (Shy) Aw … Well played, Jerry.

Heinrich: Not Jerry. Heinrich.

Tommy: My name's Tommy. Well played, Heinrich.

Heinrich: Well played, Tommy. Good shoot.

Tommy: Thanks.

Heinrich: (Sad) Today shoot football. Tomorrow shoot guns.

Tommy: Aye. (Telling story) The lads started to wander back to the trenches. But I just had to stop for one last word. (Calls to retreating Heinrich)

Tommy: Heinrich! Good luck. May God protect you and bring you home safe.

Heinrich: Good luck, Tommy.

Tommy: (Telling story)   We shook hands. The next day we were shooting one another as if nothing had happened. But that's the strangest Christmas I've ever spent, I can tell you. We had our own song for Christmas. It summed the war up in three words ...
  (Tune: *Auld Lang Syne*)

We're here because we're here because,
We're here because we're here.
We're here because we're here because,
We're here because ...

Heinrich: ...we're here.

Tommy: Having to kill someone you like. That's the most horrible history of all.[10]

10. Read more about life in the German and British armies in *Horrible Histories Terrible Trenches*.

Truce trouble

The men who played football with the enemy were told it must never happen again. Their officers said, 'You must NOT make friends with the enemy. You must kill him.'

The First World War went on until November 1918 but a Christmas truce didn't happen again.

There WAS a peaceful story from the Second World War though. It happened near the end of the war in 1944 …

• Three American soldiers became lost in a forest in Germany. The enemy were all around. One of the soldiers was badly wounded as they tried to find their allies among the trees. After three days they came upon a small cabin in the woods. It was Christmas Eve.

• A German woman, Elisabeth Vincken, had been waiting for her husband who was working in a German city. She and her 12-year-old son, Fritz, were hoping he would arrive to spend Christmas with them, but it was getting too late.

• The Vinckens had been bombed out of their home in the city and had been forced to move into an old hunting cabin in the forest. Fritz's father stayed behind to work and visited them when he could.

• There was a knock on the door. 'Father?' Fritz gasped. 'No, he wouldn't knock,' Elisabeth said. She opened the door to find two enemy American soldiers at the door. Their friend was lying in the snow. They were tattered and tired; they seemed no older than boys.

• The Americans had guns and could have forced their way in, but they didn't. Elisabeth invited them inside. They carried their wounded friend into the warm cabin. They didn't speak each other's language but they each knew a little French.

• Elisabeth started making a meal. She sent Fritz to get six potatoes and a chicken. While the meal was cooking, there was another knock on the door and Fritz went to open it. Who was it

104

this time? It was four armed German soldiers. Giving shelter to an enemy would get Elisabeth shot.

• The Germans were lost and hungry. Elisabeth told them they could come into the warmth and eat until the food was all gone, but that there were Americans inside, and the Germans would have to leave their weapons outside and come in peacefully.

• Two of the Germans were only sixteen and one was learning to be a doctor. He patched up the wounded American. They shared the Christmas meal and slept deeply. The next morning they shared maps, shook hands and found their way back to their own armies.

The happy ending...

Years later the boy, Fritz, traced two of the American soldiers and met them again. That was the happiest day of his life. One American said, 'Your mother saved my life.' Fritz was overjoyed.

2
JANUARY

ON THE NINTH DAY OF CHRISTMAS, THE RATTUS SENT TO ME ... NINE WHISTLING BISCUITS, EIGHT SLAUGHTERED SOLDIERS, SEVEN SPOOKY STORIES, SIX SNOWY STORMS, FIVE ASSASSINS, FOUR WORKHOUSE PAUPERS, THREE ROASTED DORMICE, TWO BOMBS A-DROPPED, AND A HORR-I-BLE HIS-TOR-EE.

TREATS AND TOYS

CHRISTMAS IS A TIME FOR TOYS. I'M SURE YOU ALL OPEN THEM AS FAST AS YOU CAN ON CHRISTMAS MORNING AND TRY TO MAKE THEM LAST ALL DAY BEFORE THEY BREAK.

Buttons on board

Children and grown-ups in the Middle Ages played cards and dominoes, draughts and dice. Even board games were like war games. Chess was a popular game to play. The chief piece on the chessboard was the king and the aim was to capture the enemy king – just like in a war.

A game called Merelles was well-loved among medieval children. Try it for yourself. If you have no counters, do what the children did hundreds of years ago and use buttons.

MERELLES

You will need:
Two players
Ten counters - five of one colour and five of another
A board to play on. Draw the pattern in the picture below onto cardboard to make your playing board.

How to play:
1. Each player has five counters of one colour.
2. Each takes a turn to put a counter on a spot. The aim is to put three counters in a row.
3. If all the counters are on the board then each takes a turn to move one of their counters. A player can move to any open spot next to their counter's first position.
4. The first to get three of their colour in a row is the winner.

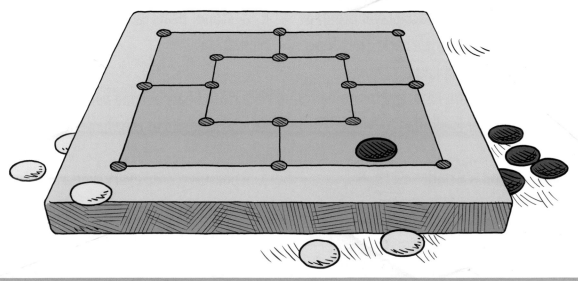

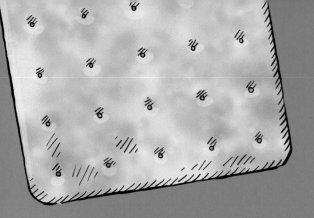

Vile Victorian games

Victorian families were often large. There was no television or radio to keep the children amused on Christmas Day so 'parlour games' were popular on long winter evenings or at parties.

A silly one you may like to try was called 'Whistling Biscuits'

WHISTLING BISCUITS

You will need:
Two teams of three or more
Two cracker biscuits for every player

How to play:
1. The two teams face each other.
2. On a signal, Player One on each team eats his or her cracker biscuits as quickly as they can.

3. When their mouth is empty enough they whistle.
4. The whistle is a signal for Player Two to eat their biscuits, then whistle.

The winning team is the one where all the players have whistled.

AND IF YOU'VE EVER TRIED TO WHISTLE AFTER EATING A CRACKER YOU'LL FIND IT HARD. YOU'LL SPIT CRUMBS OVER THE TABLE AND SPRAY BISCUIT IN SOMEONE'S FACE ... A BIT LIKE YOUR NORMAL TABLE MANNERS, EH?

Foul football

One Christmas game you would NOT want to play in medieval times was football. When the Christmas holidays came around, the menfolk of the town would enjoy a game against the village down the road. But there were no real rules, except 'Get the ball over your enemy's line.'

It was a crazy Christmas fight. The trouble was that everyone carried a knife at their belt for mealtimes. Many medieval players died falling on their own knives. One writer at the time said:

'THERE ARE NO RULES THAT I CAN TELL. THE MAN WITH THE BALL MUST RUN WITH IT FOR HIS LIFE. EVERY PLAYER LIES IN WAIT TO KNOCK DOWN THE OTHER PLAYERS OR PUNCH THEM ON THE NOSE. SOMETIMES THEIR NECKS ARE BROKEN, SOMETIMES THEIR BACKS, SOMETIMES THEIR LEGS, SOMETIMES THEIR ARMS, SOMETIMES ONE PART IS THRUST OUT OF JOINT, SOMETIMES THE NOSES GUSH OUT WITH BLOOD. FOOTBALL ENCOURAGES ENVY AND HATRED ... SOMETIMES FIGHTING, MURDER AND A GREAT LOSS OF BLOOD.'

So not a lot changes then.

OF COURSE ADULTS LOVE TOYS, TOO AND THEY HAVE LOTS OF FUN PLAYING WITH THEM. GROWN-UP TOYS ARE BIGGER THAN THE ONES YOU MIGHT PLAY WITH, AND SOMETIMES THEY CAN TURN REALLY HORRIBLE...

Full steam ahead...

The Georgian Age (1720 – 1837) was the time of the 'Industrial Revolution,' when there were hundreds of inventions that would change the world.

One of the greatest of these was the steam engine. The man who put a steam engine on wheels and started the railway age was from Cornwall and his name was Richard Trevithick.

His first try with his new toy was not a train running on rails. It was a steam car ... and it ended in a little Christmas disaster.

On Christmas Eve 1801 Trevithick decided to try out his new steam engine near the town of Camborne. The steam car was missing a couple of useful things we like to have on our cars today – it had no brakes and no steering.

It ran well enough in a straight line but lasted as long as the Trevithick family Christmas turkey. He tried it again a few days later on the rutted road outside Cambourne. The ruts kept it on the road at first but then it lurched sideways and ended up in a ditch. The driver, Andrew Vivian (Trevithick's cousin), jumped out safely. A local engineer said...

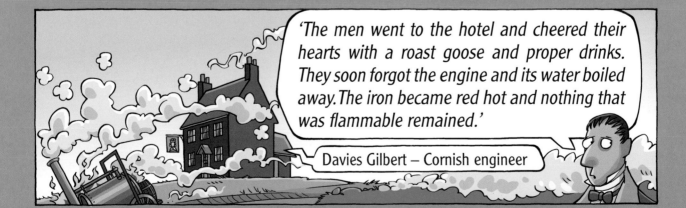

'The men went to the hotel and cheered their hearts with a roast goose and proper drinks. They soon forgot the engine and its water boiled away. The iron became red hot and nothing that was flammable remained.'

Davies Gilbert – Cornish engineer

HISTORIAE QUAE FOEDAE SUNT

2 JANUARY
On this horrible day in history ...

1911

In 1911, the East End of London is a rough place to live. There is always a lot of violence. A policeman said:

The men are not human, they are wild beasts. No law runs in these streets. The police only come when there is a bad row and they are sent for. No policeman would go alone. When called he waits for at least one other.'

It starts before Christmas when the police go to arrest burglars and three officers are killed. (The burglar is also killed because his clumsy friends shoot him in the back as they try to put bullets into the policemen.) The gang get away.

On 2 January the police are told the gang that killed the policemen are hiding in a house in Sydney Street. A hundred police surround the area. It is like a castle siege in the olden days – the

police daren't go in and the gang can't get out.

The minister in charge of the police sends in the army and a six-hour gun battle begins. Fire breaks out in the gang's house. The minister refuses to let the fire brigade go into Sydney Street to put out the fire.

The police and army wait for the gang to run from the front door – their rifles are all aimed at the doorway. No one comes out. When the fire has burned out, the bodies of two gangsters are found, but not the leader. He seems to have escaped.

That government minister is told he should not have gone to command the police and army himself. But he has always been a stubborn sort of man. He will go on to become the Prime Minister who leads Britain to victory in the Second World War. His name is Winston Churchill.[11]

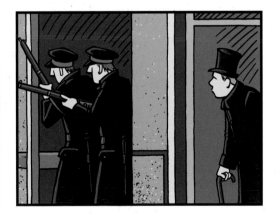

11. Read more about deadly days in London in *Horrible Histories London*.

3
JANUARY

ON THE TENTH DAY OF CHRISTMAS,
THE RATTUS SENT TO ME ...
TEN FIENDISH QUESTIONS, NINE WHISTLING
BISCUITS, EIGHT SLAUGHTERED SOLDIERS,
SEVEN SPOOKY STORIES, SIX SNOWY STORMS,
FIVE ASSASSINS, FOUR WORKHOUSE PAUPERS,
THREE ROASTED DORMICE, TWO BOMBS
A-DROPPED, AND A HORR-I-BLE
HIS-TOR-EE.

QUIZMAS TIME

CHRISTMAS WAS ALWAYS A BIG FAT TIME FOR KINGS AND QUEENS. A BIG FAT FEAST, LOTS OF DEAD BIRDS AND PLUM-PACKED PUDDINGS, FINE WINE AND PEOPLE BEING SICK. FUN WITH ACROBATS AND CLOWNS, SONG AND DANCE. THE PALACE DOGS HAD TASTY BONES TO CHEW ON AS THEY LAY IN FRONT OF ROARING LOG FIRES. WAS IT ALWAYS LIKE THAT? OF COURSE IT WASN'T. NOT ALL KINGS WERE AS KIND AS GOOD KING WENCESLAS.

How much can you guess about royal Christmases past? Take this quiz. Get 10 out of 10 and you probably cheated by looking at the answers. Get 0 out of 10 and you still scored better than Rattus.

880s

2. What Christmas thing did King Alfred invent?

a) Christmas puddings, cooked in the upturned helmets of defeated Vikings. He must have thought the Vikings were all pudding-heads!

b) Kissing under the mistletoe. He was so ugly even the queen wouldn't kiss him so he invented a rule saying you have to kiss anyone standing under mistletoe.

c) The twelve days of Christmas. Alfred's law said no free Saxon should be made to work between Christmas and Twelfth Night. (But it was fine to make your slaves work.)

1932

1. King George V sat down to give his Christmas message on the radio. He sat on his favourite chair, not the throne. What happened next?

a) The chair collapsed like Coco the Clown's car and he cried, 'God bless my soul.'

b) The king sat on a corgi and the listeners heard it yelp.

c) The listeners heard the queen say, 'Oh, George, I haven't dusted that chair.'

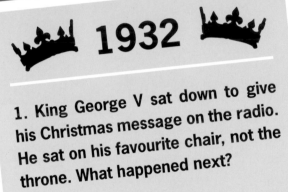

1124

3. King Henry III of England hated people who made fake copies of his coins. He kept a special punishment for them that was carried out on Christmas Day. What was it?

a) Every fake coin they had made was put in a pudding and they were forced to swallow them.

b) They were forced to run through the town with no clothes on.

c) They had their right hands and their naughty bits chopped off ... by the Bishop.

1642

4. The Members of Parliament upset King Charles I. On 4 January he stomped into the House of Commons and did what?

a) Said he would cut off five of their heads and play football with them.

b) Said he wanted five of them arrested and thrown in jail ... but the five had run away.

c) Beat five of them with his horsewhip till they ran home crying.

(They got their own back by chopping off his head eight years later.)

6. Charles I had been executed and his son, Charles II couldn't take the English throne back ... not for another 9 years. An old enemy of England decided to make Charles II THEIR king – won't THAT upset the English – so Charlie's Christmas present in 1651 was to be crowned king of which country?

a) France.

b) Turkey (well, it was Christmas).

c) Scotland.

Middle Ages

5. In Scotland, on Twelfth Night, the king gave up his throne and someone else could rule for a day. It was known as Daft Day. To be king for the day you had to find something hidden inside the Twelfth Night cake. What?

a) A bean.

b) A ring with the royal seal ... and when I say 'seal' I don't mean the fish-eating, flipper-flapping, honk-honking creature you find in the sea.

c) The queen's knickers.

Dark Ages

7. King Arthur (who MAY have been King of England or MAY be just a story) had lots of legends told about him. But which of these did he do at Christmas?

a) Pulled the sword Excalibur from a stone to prove he was the rightful king.

b) Married Queen Guinevere and lived unhappily ever after (because, as you know, she ran off with Sir Lancelot).

c) Killed 12 dragons on the 12 days of Christmas ... because a dragon a day keeps the doctor away.

2000

8. Queen Elizabeth II gave a Christmas treat to two thousand people who worked for her. What was it?

a) Free tickets to a *Horrible Histories* Christmas play.

b) Christmas puddings from a well-known supermarket.

c) A solid gold sovereign worth £85 each.

1454

9. This was a happy Christmas for King Henry VI. On Christmas Day he was suddenly cured of an illness he'd had for over a year. What had been wrong with him?

a) He stood too close to a cannon in a battle and had been deaf ever since.

b) He had sat in church to pray but a witch's curse meant his hands stayed stuck together (even though super-glue hadn't been invented).

c) He had a mental illness that meant he sat still and silent for hours like a statue, lost his memory, didn't recognise his own family and found it difficult to move without help.

1950

10. In 1297 King Edward I of England pinched the 'holy' royal 'Stone of Scotland', the 'Stone of Scone'. He moved it to Westminster Abbey. On Christmas Day 1950 what happened to it?

a) Four Scottish students stole it and took it back to Scotland where it was hidden for four months.

b) A Scottish rebel painted a tartan and slogan 'Free Scotland' in white paint on the Westminster Abbey door.

c) [illegible]

DID YOU KNOW ?
In the 1800s the royal family started going to the palatial country house at Sandringham in Norfolk for Christmas. It was a time of tricks as well as treats. One trick was to place a live lobster in somebody's bed. Lobster potty thing to do.

3 JANUARY
On this horrible day in history ...

1431

Joan of Arc was a peasant girl in France in the days when her country was being wrecked by English invaders. One day she heard angel voices telling her to become a soldier, drive the English out and put Prince Louis back on the throne of France.

She led the French to some great victories until she was captured and handed over to the English. They wanted her dead, so, on 3 January, she was handed over to a Bishop who put her on trial.

Joan was found guilty of being a witch. The punishment was to be tied to a wooden stake on top of a pile of wood. It was set on fire and she was burned alive. She was only about 19 years old.

So the evil English got what they wanted without getting the blame for killing her.

Years later she was made Saint Joan. Her story is told in a rousing song written by the talented Rattus Rattus ...

CHORUS:
Joan of Arc, what a lark,
She fought and dressed just like a bloke.
Joan of Arc, just a spark
Sent that lassie up in smoke

VERSE 1
'I was in the fields,' she said,
'The angels they were chatty!
They said I had to fight the
English!'
Her friends said she was batty!

CHORUS

VERSE 2
She went to see the Prince of France
To get a sword and breastplate
The prince he said, 'A lass like you
Should wear a woollen vest – mate!'

CHORUS

VERSE 3
But Joan she went to Orleans town
And fought and feared for nuffin'!
The nasty English all around
They got a fearful stuffin'

CHORUS

VERSE 4
At last the English captured her
They tried her with some vicars.
They said, 'You will be sorry when
That fire gets to your … kneecaps!'

CHORUS[12]

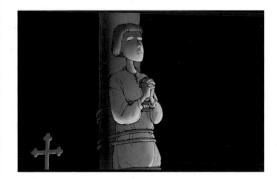

12. Read more about Joan of Arc in *Horrible Histories France*.

4
JANUARY

On the eleventh day of Christmas, the Rattus sent to me ... eleven suffering saints, ten fiendish questions, nine whistling biscuits, eight slaughtered soldiers, seven spooky stories, six snowy storms, five assassins, four workhouse paupers, three roasted dormice, two bombs a-dropped, and a horr-i-ble his-tor-ee.

SANTA AND SAINTS

GOOD OLD SAINT NICHOLAS IS KNOWN AS SANTA CLAUS FOR SHORT. YOU MAY KNOW HIM AS A JOLLY MAN IN A BIG RED SUIT, BUT DID YOU KNOW THE REAL SAINT NICHOLAS WAS A BISHOP WHO LIVED IN MYRA, TURKEY? HERE ARE SOME MORE SAVAGE STATS ABOUT THE MAN YOU CALL SANTA, AND SOME OF HIS SAINTLY FRIENDS ...

131

Saintly skeleton

1 *Bishop Nicholas died in AD 343 and was buried in Myra. But 800 years later half of his skeleton was snatched by thieves who wanted to use the bones to perform miracles.*

2 *Now half of him is in Bari, Italy. His Turkish bits ooze miraculous, rose-scented liquid each year known as 'myrrh'. You can buy flasks of the miracle stuff from the churches.*

3 *Tests on the bones show Bishop Nicholas was just 150 cm tall and had a broken nose.*

4 *As well as being patron saint of children he is also the saint of merchants. (Merchants worship him with ringing tills throughout the Christmas shopping season ... which starts in August and ends with the January sales.)*

5 *Santa is also the patron saint of thieves ... who probably call him Saint Nick. People advertize their precious presents with a treeful of lights and pile them up for any passing burglars. Thanks Santa, say the thieves.*

6 *In the Middle Ages, Saint Nicholas was always painted in pictures as a man in green. In his home town, in Turkey, there was a beautiful statue of Saint Nicholas. It was taken down by the mayor in 2005. He put up a red-suited plastic Santa Claus so the tourists would come to see the sort of Santa they expected to see. Crazy.*

So Saint Nicholas may be dead and buried but his spirit lives on as Santa Claus ... thank goodness.

Seasonal saints

Each of the saints has a day in the year when Christians are supposed to remember them. Everyone always remembers Saint Nick ... but forgets the others.

On the Twelve Days of Christmas it's time to dig up their stories and remember their horrible histories ...

Saint Stephen

Steve was one of the first Christians. The priests of Jerusalem said he was wicked and put him on trial. Did he plead for his life? No. He told them what a bunch of turnips they were. They took him out and had him stoned to death. Charming.

John the Apostle

John was one of Jesus's original twelve followers and the only one to live into old age. The Emperor Domitian had him thrown into into a cauldron of boiling oil - like a piece of haddock in your fish and chip shop - but the saint stepped out unhurt.

133

28 DECEMBER

Saint Caesarius

In AD 309 Caesarius was a Christian. The Roman rulers weren't. 'Give it up and worship the Roman gods' Emperor Galerius ordered. 'No, I won't,' Caesarius said. 'Then you'll be burned at the stake,' the Emperor said. And that's exactly what happened.

BEING AN EMPEROR, IF I SAY SOMETHING IS GOING TO HAPPEN IT USUALLY HAPPENS

29 DECEMBER

William Howard

Will was a Catholic in England. In 1678 there was supposed to be a plot to kill King Charles II. William was arrested and thrown in prison for two years. He said he never plotted against the king. The judges didn't believe him. William was taken out of prison and beheaded on Tower Hill in London.

30 DECEMBER

John Alcober

In 1728 John was sent to China as a missionary. He pretended to be a water-seller so the Chinese wouldn't kill him. He once climbed into a tree and started saying his evening prayers. A friend was hiding in the same tree and joined in prayer. A shock for John. He nearly fell off his twig. In 1746 he was caught, thrown into prison and strangled to death.

PEAR TREE PRAYER TREE

31 DECEMBER

Saint Columba of Sens

When Columba was 16 the Emperor Aurelian was killing Christians. So she ran away from her home in Spain and went to northern France. In AD 273 she was caught and thrown in prison. It looked as if she would be thrown to the killer bears in the arena. But when a Roman guard attacked her it was a bear that protected her – attacking the guard and saving her life. The Romans beheaded her in the end.

THAT'S LIFE – BEAR TODAY, GONE TOMORROW

1 JANUARY

Saint Telemachus

The Romans loved to watch gladiators chop one another up in the arena. Telemachus thought it was cruel and wicked. In the middle of a fight he stepped into an arena and told them to stop. The crowd were so upset they stoned him to death. But the Emperor Honorius DID put a stop to gladiator fights – that's what you call a result, Telemachus.

2 JANUARY

Saint Basi of Caesarea

This saint brings gifts to children every 1 January in Greece – everywhere else Father Christmas arrives on Christmas Eve (24 December). On St Basil's Day families serve 'vasilopita', a rich bread baked with a coin inside. Don't forget to save a place at the table for Saint Basil. Just mind you don't break a tooth on that coin.

3 JANUARY

Saint Gordius

Another Christian who really asked for it was Gordius. He had been a Roman soldier then decided it would be a holy idea to shed some blood for Jesus. So he went off to the arena and told the Roman Governor, 'I am a Christian, kill me.' And the governor had Gordius hacked down with swords.

4 JANUARY

Thomas Plumtree

Elizabeth I, the Tudor terror, was on the throne. She was having Catholics tortured and executed willy-nilly. Thomas joined a revolt against Bad Bess but was captured when the rebellion failed. He was told he could go free if he gave up the Catholic Church. He refused and so he was hanged in Durham Castle.

5 JANUARY

Charles of Mount Argus

This Dutch priest worked in Ireland where he was famous for curing sick people. A 12-year-old boy who lost the use of his leg was blessed by Saint Charles. In a few minutes the boy was walking up and down outside his house. A miracle. Crooks started selling bottles of water and said it was Charles's holy water. That got him banished to England for a few years. On 5 January 1893 he was not able to cure his old age and he died.

Deadly Dates

Of course many famous people in history have had birthdays or deathdays at Christmas time. Some of them came to sticky ends. But can you match the person to the horrible thing that happened to them?

CHARACTER AND DATE	STICKY END
1. Emperor Leo V – died 25 Dec 820 – he …	a. … was blinded on his 11th birthday by the man he shared the throne with.
2. King Richard II – born Twelfth Night 1367 – he …	b. … died from eating too many peaches.
3. Emperor John IV Laskaris – born 25 December 1250 – he …	c. … was assassinated by killers disguised as monks and chopped in a church.
4. King John of England – born Christmas Eve 1166 – he …	d. … fought the last great battle on British soil … and lost. He fled disguised as an Irish maid.
5. Bonnie Prince Charlie – born New Year's Eve 1720 – he …	e. … was thrown into the prison of Pontefract Castle and left to starve to death.

Answers:

1-c Emperor Leo forced Emperor Michael to hand over the throne and then he threw Michael in jail. But Michael had friends who wanted him back as emperor. They disguised themselves as monks and crept into the church where Leo was. It was gloomy in there, and they killed a priest by mistake.

Leo grabbed a cross and lashed out at the killers but he dropped it when they chopped off his arm. They cut him into pieces and dumped the bits in the snow outside. They rushed off to free Michael but couldn't find the key to his chains. (The key was in the pocket of the dead emperor in the snow.) Michael had to be crowned wearing leg irons.

2-e Henry IV said the English crown should be his. He told the English that King Richard II agreed and Richard gave up the throne – probably a lie. Richard was shut away in a dungeon and not seen again alive. The story goes that he was left to starve to death. There were stories that he was still alive and rebels were making trouble. His body was put on show in St Paul's Cathedral so no one would rebel to set him free.

3-a John was emperor of the Eastern Roman Empire and took the throne when he was just seven years old. He had to share power with his cousin Michael VIII. Michael grew tired of sharing power so had John blinded. The law said a blind person could not be emperor so John lost his throne.

Michael VIII ordered ten of his enemies to be tied together, loaded with sheep guts and poo, and led through the city. The enemy leader was smacked in the mouth with sheep's livers. A cruel rule.

4-b King John is famous for signing the Magna Carta (Great Charter) which gave away the power of the king. He signed it on the island of Runnymede in the River Thames.

He was a king who upset everyone but especially the monks. And the monks wrote the history books so they wrote that John was a rotten, evil king … well they would, wouldn't they? Even the poets sang tales of brave Robin Hood fighting evil King John. It's possible that not all the stories are true – some histories said John died from eating too many peaches, but other reports say he ate poisoned plums or drank poisoned ale.

5-d Charlie had led a Scottish army to invade England in 1745. He thought he should have been King of Britain instead of King George. He was beaten and had to run away back to Scotland. He was cornered on the Isle of Benbecula in the Outer Hebrides. There a brave woman called Flora Macdonald helped him to escape the soldiers who were searching for him. She dressed Prince Charlie as an Irish maid, Betty Burke, and sailed off in a small boat. The Prince escaped but Flora was locked in the Tower of London for a year for helping him. They should have changed his name to Betty Prince Charlie.

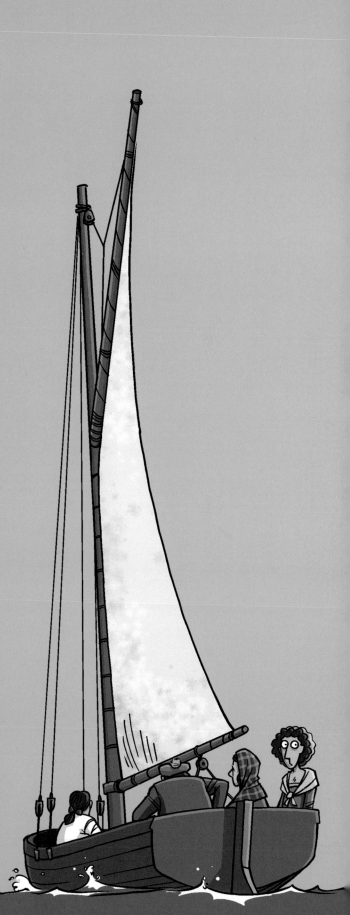

4 JANUARY
On this horrible day in history …

871

The Vikings have been roaming the seas for over a hundred years and we have seen monasteries mashed and powerless peasant villages pillaged.

When the Saxons decide to fight back the Vikings send armies to invade. The invaders settle in the town of Reading and build an earth fortress. They are attacked by a Saxon army led by King Ethelred of Wessex and his brother, Alfred the Great.

On this day in 871 the Saxons are beaten back with so much blood spilled that Reading turns reddish.

A lot of Vikings die too, but their forces will march out of the fort and chase the Saxons till Ethelred is killed. There is only young Alfred left to lead the smashing Saxon forces.

For a few years he will have to pay the Vikings to go away.

After seven years he is ready to fight back but is defeated again and has to hide.

That is where the famous story about Alfred and baking comes from. It is said that he was given shelter by a peasant woman who didn't know he was the Saxon king. She left him to watch some cakes she had cooking on the fire. Alfred was too busy thinking about the Viking wars and accidentally let the cakes burn.

Alfred will go on to become a great king. In the end the Vikings will be defeated, but Reading is one of the worst days of Christmas in his life.[13]

13. Read more about the Vikings in *Horrible Histories Vicious Vikings*.

5
JANUARY

ON THE TWELFTH DAY OF CHRISTMAS, THE RATTUS SENT TO ME...
TWELVE GUILLOTINES, ELEVEN SUFFERING SAINTS, TEN FIENDISH QUESTIONS, NINE WHISTLING BISCUITS, EIGHT SLAUGHTERED SOLDIERS, SEVEN SPOOKY STORIES, SIX SNOWY STORMS, FIVE ASSASSINS, FOUR WORKHOUSE PAUPERS, THREE ROASTED DORMICE, TWO BOMBS A-DROPPED, AND A HORR-I-BLE HIS-TOR-EE.

TWELFTH NIGHT FRIGHTS

TWELFTH NIGHT MARKS THE END OF THE CHRISTMAS PERIOD, AND IT WAS TRADITIONAL TO HAVE PARTIES AND TO PLAY PRACTICAL JOKES ON FRIENDS AND NEIGHBOURS. DON'T TRY THESE AT HOME, UNLESS YOU WANT TO BE IN TROUBLE UNTIL NEXT CHRISTMAS!

Baffling baking

- Live birds were sometimes hidden in an empty pie dish and a pie crust was put over the top. The birds would fly away when the pie was cut open … just like in the nursery rhyme 'Sing A Song of Sixpence' which says, '… when the pie was opened the birds began to sing.' (Unless your friend sticks the knife in too deep … the birdies won't be doing a lot of chirping after that.)

- In the south of the USA a King Cake is made for Twelfth Night, with a bean or sometimes a china or plastic model of baby Jesus baked inside it. Whoever finds it in their slice of cake is crowned king (hopefully their reign doesn't end quickly by choking on the bean or the baby!). In Louisiana in the 1800s the custom was made a bit messier. Any time the king took a sip of his drink, all the other guests at the table would shout 'Le roi boit!' (The king drinks.) If you forgot to shout this out, you'd have your face made dirty and smeared with food by everyone else at the party!

THE PIE'S THE LIMIT!

146

Back to the Bible

The Bible tells the story of the baby Jesus, born in a stable. It also says that Wise Men followed a star in the East and brought the holy baby three gifts. (It doesn't say there were THREE Wise Men ... just three gifts: gold, frankincense and myrrh. So there could have been 30 Wise Men, or even three hundred, but it would have been a bit of a squash to get them all in the stable.)

The story goes ...

In the time of King Herod, wise men from the East came to Jerusalem, asking, 'Where is the child who has been born King of the Jews? For we saw his star at its rising, and have come to honour Him.'

When King Herod heard this, he was frightened, and all Jerusalem with him; calling together all the chief priests and scribes of the people, he asked them where the new king was to be born.

They told him, 'In Bethlehem of Judea'. Then Herod secretly called for the Wise Men and learned from them the exact time the star had appeared. Then he sent them to Bethlehem, saying, 'Go and look carefully for the child; and when you have found Him, bring me word so that I may also worship Him.'

When they had heard the king, the Wise Men set out; and there, ahead of them, went the star that they had seen at its rising, until it stopped over the place where the child was.

When they saw that the star had stopped, they were overcome with joy. On entering the house, they saw the child with Mary His mother; and they knelt down before Him. Then, opening their treasure chests, they offered Him gifts of gold, frankincense, and myrrh.

But they had been warned in a dream not to return to Herod, so they went home to their own country by another path.

The Wise Men dodged King Herod, and Joseph fled to Egypt with his wife and child. That may have saved the life of Jesus. But it cost the lives of many other children. The Bible goes on to say …

'When Herod realized that he had been tricked by the Wise Men, he was furious, and he gave orders to kill all the boys in Bethlehem and around the town who were two years old and under.'

So the Christmas story starts with a murder plot … because Herod did NOT plan to 'worship' the baby Jesus. He planned to give him the chop … and I don't mean the lamb chop.

Carol confusion

If the Wise Men came from 'The East' – Persia, India and Arabia – then they would probably have had to cross deserts on camels – that is the picture you usually see on Christmas cards these days.

It's a bit odd then to read a Christmas carol written by a great poet, Robert Graves, (born 1895 – 1985). His carol says …

'Three kings are here, both wealthy and wise,
Come riding far over the snow-covered ice.'

Uh? Riding over snow-covered ice? Did Graves think they lived in the Antarctic? You don't see many penguin-pulled sleighs on Christmas cards, do you? What would their presents have been? Cold, frankincense and brrrrrr?

5 JANUARY
On this horrible day in history …

1857

In France a servant called Robert-François Damiens tries to kill his king, Louis XV. On 5 January he stabs at the king as he climbs into a carriage but only gives him a scratch.

He doesn't try to run away so he is arrested and tortured. 'Who else is in your plot to kill the king?' they ask. He doesn't name anyone – probably because he acted alone. The judge says he should die by being hanged, drawn and quartered.

In fact on the day of his execution he has his hand tortured because it held the knife – it is nipped with hot pincers then burned with hot wax, lead and boiling oil. He is taken out and each arm and leg is tied to a horse. The horses are then sent to gallop off in different directions so he is torn apart. What is left is burned at the stake and the ashes scattered to the winds.

The punishment goes on for the living. Damiens's house is burned down, his brothers and sisters are ordered to change their names. His

wife, daughter and father are banished from France.

Just 35 years later the French are chopping down their lords like corn at harvest time. The French Revolution came along and the guillotine (a chopping machine) is doing what Damiens failed to do – killing a king.

He is the last man in France ever to suffer this evil execution.

Epilogue

MERRY CHRISTMAS

SO NOW YOU'VE HEARD ABOUT THE HORRIBLE CHRISTMASES IN DAYS GONE BY, LEARN FROM THEM AND MAKE SURE YOU STAY SAFE DURING THESE DANGEROUS DAYS!

HAVE A BIG, FAT HAPPY CHRISTMAS TIME BUT NEVER FORGET THE REAL CHRISTMAS MESSAGE. IT IS GIVING, NOT GETTING, THAT MATTERS. AND, OF COURSE, IT IS ALL ABOUT THE BIRTH OF JESUS. THOSE TWO THINGS ARE SUMMED UP IN THIS LITTLE POEM WHAT I WROTE ...

THE FIRST CHRISTMAS PRESENT
By
Rattus Rattus

The shepherds were watching their flock in the fields
While stars in the dark sky were flitting.
Old Thomas was carving a fine woollen doll,
While young Jim got on with his knitting …
… a scarf!

As Tommy remarked
'That's a big star up there!'
An angel came down with a bound.
Old Tom dropped the doll while young Jim dropped a stitch
And the sheep ran around and around …
… in circles!

The angel just folded his wings and he grinned,
'Hi, lads, get along to the tavern!
A baby is born, it's the child of the Lord,
Take some prezzies and let the babe have 'em!
… Please!'

'We cannot do that! You great feathered fool!'
Old Tom stood and started to shout.
'The sheep'll get got by the greedy old wolf!'
'Don't worry, lads, I'll sort him out …'
Said the angel.

But still the old man he was fussing about,
'I haven't got no gifts at all!'
But Jim said, 'I'll take him my nice woolly scarf!
And you, Tom, can give it the doll …'
… if you like.

'You're really good blokes,' the angel went on,
But don't forget Joseph and Mary.'
'He's right!' young Jim said, 'Why not take them a lamb?
That one there's all cuddly and hairy …
… and fat.'

The shepherds went trotting down Bethlehem hill
And they follow the star where it shines;
'Look at that,' Old Tom moaned, 'there's camels and kings
And they've parked them on two yellow lines
…They'll be for it.'

Now the shepherds felt shy as they crept in the back
Of the stable and saw who it were.
Three great kings stood there with their arms full of gifts,
Stuff like gold, frankincense and some myrrh …
… very posh.

Jim's small lamb went "Baa!", Mother Mary said
'Ahhhh! Come on in, put your gifts by the bed.'
'Thanks a lot,' whispered Tom, 'But our gifts aren't as grand
As them blokes with the crowns on their heads …
… they're so shiny.'

Mary loved Jimmy's scarf, it would keep the babe warm
And the lamb's wool would make her a frock.
'In fact, Joseph,' she said, 'with a fine lamb like that
We could maybe now start our own flock …
Think of that.'

Then Joseph he smiled and he said
'Very nice.' but the truth is his smile was a sham.
To be honest he had looked at the gift and he thought
Tasty chops. Or a nice leg of lamb.
… Yum! Yum! Yum!

Poor old Tom felt as sick as a six year-old chip
As he held out his wood doll so sad.
'Sorry Mary, my dear, but the chap with the wings
Never said that the babe was a lad …
… he won't want dolls!'

Mary smiled very kind at the shepherd so old
And the wood doll was really quite beautiful.
'It's the thought, not the gift, that's what matters, you know.
And who knows, but it might come in useful …'
… She was right!

Meanwhile, back in the palace, bad King Herod had heard
Of a new king, and he was real cross.
'I will send out you men for to find him and snatch him,
And make jolly sure he gets lost …
… for good.'

When the shepherds returned to their sheep in the hills,
Leaving Joseph and Mary in danger,
Two great soldiers burst in to the cave the next day
And they snatched up the babe from the manger …
… that was that.

But Joseph just laughed and his wife Mary smiled
As she slipped the babe from her cloak creases.
And the soldiers so dim never knew to this day,
'Twas the wood doll that they'd chopped to pieces …
… served them right.

So when Christmas time comes we remember the first gifts
From rich kings and from shepherds in tatters.
And the words of the lady, so wise when she said,
'It's the thought, not the gift, that's what matters …
Merry Christmas!'